UNDERSTANDING THE BRITISH

A HILARIOUS GUIDE FROM APOLOGISING TO WIMBLEDON

ADAM FLETCHER

A SHORT DISCLAIMER ABOUT NAMES

Have you noticed that Britain has more identities than a serial impostor, more titles than a third-world despot, and more names than a Portuguese midfielder?

Yes, I thought you probably had.

Britain, Great Britain, Team GB, the United Kingdom, the Commonwealth—names that mean different things, that refer to distinct groups, nations, cultures, and islands yet are applied interchangeably, haphazardly, and (almost always) incorrectly. It's all a bit of a mess, really, this "British" thing.

A nice mess.

A polite mess.

A mess with a side plate of biscuits.

But a mess nonetheless.

Especially since so many of us prefer to identify not as British but as English, Scottish, Welsh, or Northern Irish—all of whom think differently, act differently, and curse differently from each other.

Accordingly, it's simply impossible to do justice to the

complexity of a culture that can't even agree on the basics, like what it's calling itself. So, in this little guide, I've reserved the right to use all our different names interchangeably, inaccurately, and with limited respect for the distinct cultural differences of the nations, islands, and political bodies that make up the United Kingdom of Great Britain, Northern Ireland, and its Crown Overseas Dependencies (our longest, most inclusive, least bumper-sticker friendly nomenclature). I'll call us a people when we're really a diverse collection of peoples. I'll call us a nation when we're several. I'll call us united when we squabble more than drunk reality TV stars in a hot tub.

And with that, let's begin.

NORTHERN
IRELAND

SCOTLAND

THE NORTH

THE MIDLANDS

WALES

GREATER
LONDONIA

CHAPTER I

"In a nutshell"

The Basics

BE NICE

My brother mentions that he and his girlfriend need a coffee table. That evening, my mum is browsing a website where local people list things for sale and finds an attractive-looking specimen. She sends the link to my brother. The table costs a whole five pounds. He agrees that it fits the accepted definition of a bargain. But it's a bit far away for him.

"No problem," says Mum, wanting to be nice. "We'll pick it up for you and bring it over."

She calls the man selling it. It's a fifteen-minute drive to what turns out to be an insalubrious part of town. She's alone. She knocks on the front door. No one answers. She gets back in the car and calls the man.

"I'm home," he says. "Come around the back."

She walks down a dark alley to the back of the house. There she finds a tall metal staircase leading to a first-floor door. A man's silhouette is visible behind its glass pane. Her stomach knots. She gulps. She goes back to the car and drives the fifteen minutes home.

Her phone beeps as she drives. The man has sent a text

message. He's annoyed. He's waited in especially for her; she's the third person to let him down, he says.

Probably because of your creepy alley, staircase, and murderous vibe, she wants to tell him, but doesn't, because that wouldn't be nice. She agrees to try again the next night. The table is a bargain, after all. She'll take my dad with her.

The next night finds my parents on the couch, tired from work. "Do we have to go?" my dad asks.

"I told the man I would," she replies.

Dad *sinods* (an innovative mixture of both a sigh and a nod, perfected over several decades of marriage). Reluctantly they put on shoes and wrap into coats and climb wearily into the car.

Mum reverses it out of the curved driveway.

"Watch it," Dad says. "You're going to hit the neighbour's wall."

"I've reversed out of this driveway a thousand times, you idiot! I think I know what I'm doing."

Crunch.

The car and the neighbour's wall become intimately acquainted. My parents swear at each other, and the wall, and marriage, and the five-pound table. But it's too late not to go now—they told the man they were coming, and they don't want to let him down again. It wouldn't be nice. So, they drive the fifteen minutes back to the insalubrious part of town.

"Can you go in?" Mum asks. "I get a bad feeling from this guy."

Dad trudges down the dark alleyway. The man's silhouette is visible up on the first floor. Dad shudders and looks back at my mother in the car. He compares the potential inconvenience of being murdered with the relief of never having to do another of her chores again.

6

It's worth it, he decides.

The door opens, releasing a thick cloud of cigarette smoke into the frosty winter night. A man with a neck tattoo of a topless mermaid beckons him inside. The door closes behind them with a clunk. The apartment is as dark and cluttered as any hermit's hovel.

In the centre of the room sits a tatty, pockmarked brown coffee table. It has been some time since it has experienced kindness. The photo the man used in the listing might be of this table, but several decades ago.

Inspecting the table, Dad concludes that it's overpriced at five pounds: an achievement. He doesn't say this, of course, because it wouldn't be nice. And the man has eyes that swivel like fishes and a kitchen that's probably full of sharp knives. To avoid making a scene, Dad compliments the table extensively, pays the five pounds, and leaves with his life, a horrible five-pound table, and many future chores ahead. It's a high price, but at least he has avoided making a scene.

For us Brits, there's nothing worse than making a scene.

He carries the table back down to the car, glad the ordeal is over.

"What were you thinking?" Mum asks incredulously as he manhandles it into the back seat.

"I was thinking I just want an easy life," he says, slamming the rear door.

The next day, they drive the car to the mechanic. The good news is that the dent and scratch inflicted by my mother's bad driving and the neighbour's wall can be fixed. The bad news is it'll cost two hundred pounds. My parents throw sharp words at each other. Some of them cut. They drive thirty minutes to my brother's place, mostly in silence, to present him with his new coffee table and the completion of their good deed.

They have been nice. No one can dispute this.

They show my brother the table. He doesn't like it. Neither does his girlfriend. They don't say this, of course, because that wouldn't be nice—but it's clear from the amount that they compliment it, which is a lot and so wholly out of proportion to its actual niceness.

My brother hands my mum a twenty-pound note. She gives him a ten in return and then asks my dad if he has a five? He checks. He doesn't. She checks her pockets. Neither does she. Time passes. The search is fruitless. "Don't worry about it," she says, handing him back his original twenty-pound note, forgetting she has already given him a ten.

They leave. My mother drives. She is extra careful reversing.

Getting my brother this table, a table no one likes, has cost my parents a two-hundred-pound car-repair bill, several arguments, three round trips, several awkward situations in an alleyway, and a dozen future hours of marriage counselling. Oh, and on top of that, they also *paid my brother* ten pounds to take it from them.

They can't tell my brother any of this, of course, since they don't want him to feel guilty, and it might be awkward. But they tell me. Mum finds it funny, Dad not so much. "I just wanted to do something nice," she says, for the twelfth time. Dad sinods. He can't argue with that. Amongst my curious people, nothing counts for more.

Other cultures would probably disagree with that statement. They know the road to hell is paved with good intentions. Well, so do we milky-tea drinkers. We see how much extra hassle all this niceness is, how much it complicates in the aim of simplifying, yet we don't care. Some things are more important than efficiency. We don't care for outcomes; we think results are overrated. We're into more ephemeral, metaphysical things: having a good heart, being a nice person, doing good deeds, not making a fuss. If that leads us to hell—a very polite, civil hell in which we're to spend eternity being roasted in the fires of our own misplaced good intentions—so be it. My mum sums it up best when talking about me and my siblings: "It makes no difference to me if you're bin men or brain surgeons. All that has ever been important to me is that you're nice."

The next time my parents go to my brother's house the table is gone. No one ever mentions it again. It wouldn't be nice.

Welcome to Britain.

THE IDEAL OF BRITISHNESS

There's a phenomenon called the Disneyland Effect. It dictates that your first experience of something sets the benchmark against which subsequent experiences must compare. If that first experience isn't representative—say you win the lottery your first time playing, fall in love on your first date, or the plane crashes on your first flight—you end up with a distorted idea of normalcy for it.

An oft-cited Disneyland Effect experience is the safari.

For most of us, our first and formative safari experience is an animal-themed ride in an amusement park. We sit in a bright-blue plastic boat floating around a simulation African savannah and for three intense minutes are bombarded by exotic animatronic animals: lions growl an inch from your face, zebras gallop along beside you, a family of meerkats dances on the shell of a giant turtle as tribal music blaring from speakers hidden in bushes builds to its thrilling crescendo. Safaris, you think, as you exit via the gift shop. *Wonderful.*

So, you book an actual safari.

It's then that you learn that an actual safari, you know, like in Africa, is getting up at dawn to spend six hours being bounced on your coccyx in the back of a jeep and swallowing mouthfuls of dust while being snacked on by squadrons of mosquitoes—just to glimpse one solitary giraffe sleeping under a tree.

Does that giraffe sing or dance? Like heck.

The "Circle of Life"? Shove off, Elton.

You decide that maybe you like the artificial, sanitised version of safaris better than the real thing.

The following, I think, is a pretty good summary of most people's experience with the British.

Britain: the brand, the idea, the myth, the theme-park experience? *Wonderful.* A joyous pop-culture rollercoaster through history: the Mini, James Bond, swinging-sixties London, Monty Python, dancing to the Stones, Harry-Potter-reading marathons, summers of Wimbledon.

Not all nationalities work their citizens equally—some exert higher demands. Italians get to be free-feeling, free-speaking, free-gesticulating passionate communicators. Mexicans get to sleep all afternoon, wear sombreros, and drink tequila. If a German makes one joke a week, she's the office comedian. If an American can find France on a map, he's considered multicultural. If Australians put on shoes, people assume it's their wedding day.

We Brits don't have it so easy. Popular culture is not only your first experience with us, your Brit safari, it's also our first experiences of ourselves, too. In school, at home, on TV, through the music coming from our radios, the whitewashed empire of our history books, the self-righteous tone of our newspapers—we're indoctrinated, just as you're indoctrinated with the Idea of Britishness.

More than that, perhaps: the *Ideal* of Britishness.

We're taught that we're something special. We're the

direct descendants of the most successful empire of all time, after all. The occupiers of the dead centre of the world map. Creators of the planet's lingua franca. Birthplace of Shakespeare. The Beatles. Yes, *those* Beatles. All four of them. We're hit-it-out-of-the-park cultural overachievers. We've sold our cultural mythology hard, and no one has bought more of it than we have.

Because of this, we feel a pressure to always, always, be funny; to speak perfect Oxford English; to remain stiff-upper-lipped in adversity; to say sorry for even the slightest of provocations; to not be a burden, a bother, or an inconvenience; to be self-reliant. To understand the British, you have to understand how much we're struggling with the disconnect between the values of our don't-make-a-fuss culture and the needs of us as individuals, between the Ideal of Britishness and the execution of Britishness. You have to understand everyday life on a small, overcrowded, damp collection of islands showing their age and, perhaps, a little past their cultural and economic prime.

It's all a bit overwhelming and intimidating and mostly impossible. So, cut us just a little slack, will you? Hopefully, in time, we'll learn to do just the same.

How we're supposed to be   How we are

4

THE HIERARCHY OF BRITISH NEEDS

With apologies to Mr Maslow

I know what you're probably thinking: why is tea so damn high? Tea is obviously a basic British need, like oxygen, swearing, and chocolate biscuits. Tea should be at the bottom. And it would have been were it not for the inflexible shape of pyramids and thus my need to find a three-letter word for the summit. Please forgive this flagrant distortion of truth.

5

THE MASK OF CIVILITY

Remember the hit nineties movie *The Mask*, starring Jim Carrey? Carrey plays meek, mild-mannered bank clerk Stanley Ipkiss—a man transformed when he puts on a mysterious, powerful green mask that allows him to shake off his anxieties, grab life by its metaphorical balls, and win the love of a blonde woman in a skin-tight red dress.

Well, we Brits also wear a special mask every (sober) minute of our existence. If you want to understand us, to successfully interact with us without offending us or getting mocked mercilessly by us, you'll need to put it on, too.

It's called the Great British Mask of Civility.

They give them out at immigration, I think.

Wearing it won't make you feel less anxious, or be less meek, or win the love of blonde women in skin-tight red dresses. Because when we Brits watched *The Mask*, we couldn't identify with the ballsy, extroverted green guy who got the girl. The guy vulgarly doing whatever he wanted all the time; drawing attention to himself; not soldiering bravely on, without complaint, doggedly resigned to accepting his lot in life.

To be honest, we thought he was a bit of a dick.

Instead, we identified with mild-mannered, long-suffering Stanley Ipkiss. That guy we could really get behind. With our Mask of Civility on, we're just like him.

Wearing it tightens your brow in an expression of apology for having had the audacity to exist, relaxes your mouth into a soft, pensive smile on which the word *sorry* sits ready, and adds a twinkle to the corner of your eye, suggesting wit lurks ready around every sentence's corner.

This mask might sound bad to you but it's not. It's just a cultural adaptation, a coping mechanism, a way of making interactions between ourselves easier. Because while Britain is not as rule laden and passionately indirect as Japan, we too live on a tiny, overcrowded island. Except on ours, water keeps falling uninvited from the sky; we can't get a hospital appointment for six months; house prices are at record levels and rising; the train is delayed—AGAIN; and a day when the temperature tops twenty-five degrees Celsius is declared a national holiday.

Ugh.

Which is why, in small, petty moments, we need our Mask to help block the connection between our feelings and our face. To help us remain polite and civil. All our feelings are still there, underneath. We're just going to let them out differently, in subtext and humour mostly.

But let's not get ahead of ourselves.

The Mask of Civility

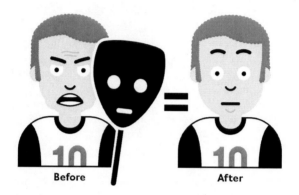

Before   **After**

SAY SORRY

Y ou probably think you know how to be sorry and when to apologise, don't you?

You might even think expressing regret is easy. You just go do a little something wrong, feel bad, then ask for forgiveness by saying the magic word—*sorry*—and you're absolved.

No. *Stop*. You're doing it wrong.

My culture understands that sorry is not a mop you can use to clean up all your indiscretions. Sorry is more powerful than that. Sorry is a way of life. A worldview. A dogma. We know we should apologise before we've even done anything wrong. Keep Calm and Carry On might have become our national motto, but it should really be Say Sorry Carry on Feeling Guilty and Come Back and Apologise Six More Times Just to Be Sure.

Not as good on a poster though, that one.

If you're unsure when you should be saying sorry, Team GB style, please consult the following handy flow chart.

Should you apologise?

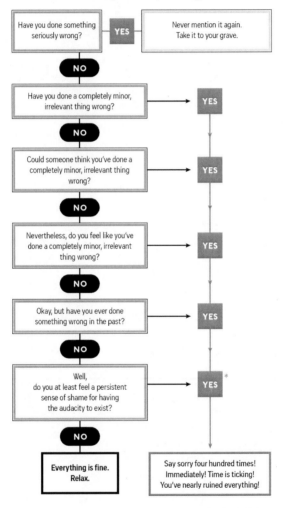

Have you done something seriously wrong? — **YES** → Never mention it again. Take it to your grave.

NO ↓

Have you done a completely minor, irrelevant thing wrong? → **YES**

NO ↓

Could someone think you've done a completely minor, irrelevant thing wrong? → **YES**

NO ↓

Nevertheless, do you feel like you've done a completely minor, irrelevant thing wrong? → **YES**

NO ↓

Okay, but have you ever done something wrong in the past? → **YES**

NO ↓

Well, do you at least feel a persistent sense of shame for having the audacity to exist? → **YES** *

NO ↓

Everything is fine. Relax.

Say sorry four hundred times! Immediately! Time is ticking! You've nearly ruined everything!

* CONGRATULATIONS, YOU ARE BRITISH!

CHAPTER 2

"If you'll pardon my French"

Our Worldview

DON'T BE A BURDEN OR A BOTHER

I'm at Schönefeld Airport, in Berlin, waiting for my flight to London Stansted. An extremely old man enters the gate. All the gate's seats have been taken by Germans who planned ahead. And me, three-quarters German after eight years of living in Berlin. The man shuffles over on his rubbish, worn-out, aged limbs. He crumples next to the wall like an accordion.

He lets out a sigh of the defeated. I rise from my chair. "Would you like to sit down?" I ask. (I've kept the part of me that needs to be nice. It's all my mum wanted, after all.)

He smiles. "No, no, I'm fine." He says, with a slight Liverpudlian accent.

"Please, sit down. I insist."

"No, it's fine, really. I don't want to be a bother."

"Sit down—please. It's no bother," I say, a little bit aggressively because my three-quarters Germanness detests inefficiency and indecision as one detests early mornings and dental work.

I push him down into my chair with the strength of my gaze. "Oh, hmmh, well, if you insist. But I really don't want to be a bother . . ." he says, dropping into the seat like a sack of potatoes falling off a cupboard.

From that seat, he smiles up at me.

I smile down at him, pretending I'm enjoying leaning against the wall.

He pretends he's enjoying the seat.

We're both lying.

He is having a wretched time despite his newfound recline. For he knows he's a burden, a bother, a nuisance, an inconvenience. All traits in direct opposition to our highest cultural values. We're supposed to be the *stiff-upper-lip-pers*; the *keep calm and carry on-ers*; the *Dunkirk spirit-ers*.

Accordingly, we love to martyr ourselves, not be martyred for. I'm sure the extra comfort he feels for sitting is offset by this guilt. Perhaps he has broken even. Perhaps he is now actually comfort negative.

I'm also having a worse time on the wall. Yet we continue to smile at each other as if this is one of the better days of our existence. Then it happens. I feel a twinge in my back. But I don't want to move. If I move he's going to see that I'm uncomfortable and he's going to know he's the reason why.

I'd bother him.

My discomfort rises. The pain in my back intensifies. I grit my teeth but don't move. Pain shoots down my leg. I tilt like an Italian tourist attraction. I grit my teeth harder. A bead of sweat runs down my forehead. I smile warmly at the man, as warmly as I can between the jolts of pain. Is this what labour feels like?

This probably isn't what labour feels like, I decide. I'm prone to melodrama.

Eventually, unable to take it anymore, I shift down onto my haunches to rest. In the process, I let out an involuntary yelp. The man notices. He knows he's the cause of this involuntary yelp. It's like a dagger in his heart. The lights in his eyes go out. "Can we swap back?" he asks.

"No, I'm fine. I like standing," I say unconvincingly, while squatting.

His head tilts. "Do you? Well, I like standing, too. It's no bother," he replies, throwing another lie on the pile.

They announce we can board the plane. We both exhale in relief and hobble together over to the door. The ordeal is over. We are free. I leave the exchange feeling that, because of my act of kindness, both of us lost, yet everything was exactly as it should have been, and I would do it all again in a heartbeat. For this is being British: doing what's right, even if everyone loses in the process.

It's a wonder we've lasted this long as a people. I can only imagine wounded British soldiers on the beaches of Normandy, bombs exploding in the background, a field nurse rushing over to assist them, only to be waved away by a soldier lying in a pool of his own blood: "I'm fine, really. It's just a scratch."

"What?" says the nurse. "It looks to me like you're bleeding profusely."

"Oh, am I? I hadn't even noticed, to be honest. "

"If I'm not mistaken, your left leg has been blown clean off."

"Has it? Blimey. There goes a promising footballing career. Well, I think the man next to me has had *both* his legs blown off. So, deal with him first. I don't want to be any inconvenience."

"He's dead."

"Is he? Oh dear. Well, I imagine there's some paper-work involved with that? You'll need to notify people? Perhaps some light burying and whatnot? Lots to do, no doubt. Best get to it. Don't put yourself out for little old me."

8

TUTHISM

There is a miscomprehension that the UK isn't religious, perhaps because the only time you'll see us pray is when clutching a betting slip, the most devotion we show is to our football teams, and our most famous church is Charlotte Church.

Well, that's wrong.

We're acolytes, believers, and disciples, all right. It's just that we follow a secret religion. And my (admittedly anecdotal) research suggests every single British person is a member of this special religion.

It's called Tuthism.

You may have noticed that life is sometimes a little irritating. On the whole, it's good—you're happy to be here and that nachos exist and that in two days it's the weekend. Yet, there are all these in-between moments when things don't work out as you hope: when you drop chicken soup down your freshly washed trousers; when the train is late (again!) and now you'll miss your favourite TV programme of reality TV stars arguing in a hot tub; when a homeless man urinates on your new shoes; when you have ten thousand spoons and all you need is a knife.

It's in these small daily moments of frustration that we Brits turn to Tuthism and give a short prayer up to the heavens. To one man, specifically: Saint Tut—patron saint of mild inconveniences.

Just as Hare Krishnas pray by repeating the name of their god, we pray by repeating the name of our patron saint: Tut.

We really love tutting, you may have noticed.

It's hard to describe how to do it, since doing it is so natural for us. I think we come out of the womb tutting. It was hot in there. We're late. We've stuff to do. *Baby stuff.*

To make this important sound, put your tongue on the roof of your mouth then suck sharply. You should notice an immediate release of life's tension. Proof Saint Tut has worked his magic again.

After apologising, tutting is the most popular national pastime of my people. Often, if a train is delayed, the tutting on the platform takes on the religious fervour of Hajj. A chorus of polite discontent as deafening as cicadas on a summer night.

Tutting allows us to ask Saint Tut for help, and to signal our annoyance to those around us in a non-confrontational way that doesn't threaten our brittle social equilibrium. That doesn't make us too much of a bother.

Feel free to join us.

Or not.

Tsk.

9

CONBACKTATIONS

One Easter, when I was a kid, my grandparents bought me a Cadbury Creme Egg.* Being well raised, and indoctrinated in Nice, I thanked them and praised Cadbury Creme Eggs enthusiastically. After this, every time I saw them—and it was often, since they lived a mere ten houses away—they would present me with a Cadbury Creme Egg, "my favourite".

I didn't like Cadbury Creme Eggs. I didn't like them at all. They were yucky.

I never had the heart to tell them. Then too much time and too many eggs had passed.

The person who most profited from this was my friend Dan. He lived in the house opposite, loved Cadbury Creme Eggs, and had an uncanny knack for appearing at our front door, an expectant look on his face, just as my grandparents were putting on their shoes.

This farce continued for ten years.

This story and the coffee-table saga of Chapter 1, while mild, are small examples of just how conflict-avoidant we Brits are. While other cultures might solve problems head-on—a commendable ability that is as exotic to us as flight, alchemy, and cooking with spices that aren't salt and pepper—we Brits attempt to solve problems by turning our backs on them and pretending they don't exist.

We don't have confrontations. We have con*back*tations.

Problem? What problem? There's no problem. Cuppa, anyone?

I think it's precisely because our culture has no mechanism for getting out of disputes that we must be so careful not to get into them. Something as simple as an awkward conversation with a neighbour about the appropriate volume for playing Boney M's *Greatest Hits* might turn into a five-year-long passive-aggressive feud resulting in the need to check out the window every time you leave the house.

Not cool, Daddy.

I remember my family having just such a con*back*tation at one of our previous homes. A family had moved in opposite. They had two children the same age as my sister and I. My parents encouraged us to make friends with them, in the hope we'd be home less often, I think.

So, we did.

Then we discovered the two children were awful, horrible, and, perhaps even worse, *American*. But it was too late now. They lived opposite. We couldn't avoid them. And, being new to England, and so unaware of British customs, they didn't pick up on any of our subtle social cues and subtext.

Didn't spot that we didn't like them.

Kept coming around unannounced.

Ringing the bell.

Sticking their heads over the fence.

It was like a zombie (neighbour) invasion.

It culminated, one afternoon, in our hiding below the

27

windows as the two American devil children rang the bell incessantly. Being American (have I mentioned they were American?), and so unaware of even the rudimentaries of tact, they then began looking through the bungalow's windows in turn, until they spotted my mum lying on her bedroom floor, partially shrouded in a shaggy rug.

Rumbled, she had to get up and concoct a plausible story that explained why she hadn't heard the doorbell (which the elder boy had rung at least ten times) and was "sleeping" on the bedroom floor, right next to the room's actual bed, under a shaggy rug.

If anything more awkward has occurred in human history, I'm not aware of it.

My sister calls the people she gets into con*back*tations with "demons". She advises people to move towns every few years because you get to "begin again, demon free". I'm not making this up. You couldn't make this up. Fortunately, shortly after, the Americans moved out.

We threw a party to celebrate.

We didn't invite any of the neighbours.

---

*Creme Eggs are what would happen if Willy Wonka and the Oompa-Loompas got high and stumbled around the chocolate factory's canteen giggling while pushing random ingredients into an oval. More than two hundred million of these monstrosities are sold each year, to people of questionable taste, and few remaining teeth. *Hi, Dan!*

28

LOGICAL DISPUTE RESOLUTION

Dispute.

Midsize
existential crisis.

Explain
your problem
to the person
responsible.

End the conversation
with **"Sorted?"** and a
firm handshake.
Problem solved.

BRITISH DISPUTE RESOLUTION

Dispute.

Ignore
the problem.
Make tea.

Talk to the
person you have
a problem with
about the weather.

Talk to the
person you have
a problem
with about reality TV.

Spend
six months
quietly seething.

Get drunk
together.

Shout at
each other.

Say:
"Let's agree to disagree!"
Hug, bury the hatchet with
another drink (or twelve).

FAFFING

W hile I'm sitting in my parents' living room, the topic of where to go for dinner comes up. It's a predictable conversation in which we'll leisurely talk over, under, and around our true desires, teasing them out slowly using subterfuge and misdirection.

Paint dries quicker. Kyoto protocols are ratified faster.

Eventually, we'll go to the first place suggested (an hour ago). All participants know this. But, still, this polite dance must be danced. For us, an hour-long discussion of this nature, where we avoid saying things we could condense into five minutes, is not a problem per se. British culture values harmony, not efficiency. Some cultures want to do it well; we want to do nicely. A problem would only arise when my very German ex-girlfriend Annett visited. She'd be thrown, without understanding the rules, into the middle of a decorum game she didn't even know she was playing. She would see our indecision, inefficiency, and meekness as a problem to be solved. Her solution was always to step in and make the decision for everyone.

I'm solving the problem, she'd think. *She is the problem*, everyone else knew. Because what for her was an annoying trailer was for us the feature film. We even have a special word for it, for wilful acts of deliberate inefficiency: *faffing*.

Faffing is, in many ways, our worldview. It's easy to explain but takes a lifetime to truly master.

Faffing is getting up from a chair. Then forgetting why. Then sitting down again. Then talking about the weather for five minutes. Then scratching your head. Remembering you still haven't called Bill about Tuesday. Deciding if you should call Bill about Tuesday. Saying "right then" to no one in particular. Getting up to call Bill about Tuesday. *Sighing*. Striding purposefully towards the phone then swerving inexplicably into the kitchen to get a yoghurt. Eating the yoghurt while staring at a pot plant. *Where did you get that pot plant?* More importantly, *when did you last water it?* Water it. Sit back down. Forget to call Bill about Tuesday. Sigh theatrically for no reason. Get up to let the dog out. Stop at the window to make judgemental comments about the neighbour's children. Tut. Say "right then". Scratch your chin. Shout at the dog to stay out of the bushes. Stare at the pot plant. *Where did you get that pot plant? When did you last water it?* Water it. Try to remember why it was you got up. Say "right then". Go sit back down, let out a contented sigh. It's nice to be off your feet. Calculate how long you have before you must move again. Chuckle. Hear the dog scratching at the back door. *How did the dog get out?* Tut. Say "right then". Get up . . .

Faffing is the art of doing nothing, badly.

BE ONE OF THE GANG

For all human history, it has been of the utmost importance to stay part of the group, since getting exiled used to mean almost certain death. Which is why people bristle when topics like politics come up. For thousands of years, uttering the wrong word, saying the wrong god's name, swearing allegiance to the wrong tribal leader might see you hung, burnt alive, or sent off into the wilderness to die slowly in the cold, or quickly inside the mouth of a bear.

All quite rubbish endings, really.

Thankfully, those days are (mostly) behind us now, and so we're free to stick our necks out a little more in social contexts. Yet this drive to be part of a group remains deeply within us. In Britain, a collectivist culture, this is especially true. We're always monitoring and reinforcing each other's behaviour in subtle ways—the cold stare, the subtle cough, the raised brow, the well-timed "really?"—that endeavour to nudge people back into line and ensure group harmony.

You can also see it in our choice of conversation topics.

Other places have deep and meaningful conversations. We have shallow yet plentiful banalities. Britain must be one of the few places where you can get mocked for being smart; where talking about a book you read recently makes it seem as if you're showing off; where mentioning a documentary will result in someone using the word *cultured* as if it's an insult; where biking to the pub will get you branded as a hippy; where wearing slightly shiny trousers (outside of London) will mean someone in a passing car shouts "OI, Gary Glitter!" at you.

Anyone who tries to stand out, show off, boast, brag, crow, trumpet, or gloat is put back into place with the full force of our scorns, tongues, and wits. We don't have Fight Club—we have Fight Pomposity Club. When magician David Blaine fasted in a clear Perspex box suspended over the River Thames for forty-four days—for reasons best known only to himself—we did our best to distract him with abusive signs, hand gestures, trash, and golf balls. People drummed whenever he tried to sleep. A flash mob waved burgers at him. When Margaret Thatcher died, we reacted by buying "Ding Dong! The Witch Is Dead" en masse, sending it to second in the charts.

It's why we turn up at protests with polite signs saying "Down with this kind of thing!" Why when asked to name our shiny, new tax-funded research vessel, we decided on Boaty McBoatface.

Other cultures might want to stand out, but we want to fit in. To fade into the background. To keep the group together and strong.

To be one of the gang.

THE NHS

y girlfriend, Julia, tells a story about visiting a journalist friend in Cairo. It had been a year since a military coup overthrew the government there.

"How has it been since the coup d'état? Has it affected your job?" she asks her friend. They're sitting in a cafe drinking tea from unnecessarily small glasses.

Her friend looks around nervously. "Coup! Do you mean *The People's Glorious Revolution?*"

In every society, no matter how developed, liberal, and free, there are certain things you just can't say. Truths no one is willing to confront. Sacred cows one should not lead to slaughter. For the British, the National Health Service, *ahem*, I mean *The People's Glorious National Health Service*, is just such an institution. As untouchable as the Queen, Adele, Stephen Fry, Princess Diana, the BBC, and Mr Bean. "The NHS is the closest thing the English have to a national religion," said politician Nigel Lawson. I think by that that he meant it can't be criticised, it's full of false idols, and it's out of touch with the modern world.

I'd say our relationship with the NHS is nearer one might have with an abusive spouse; the worse it treats us, the more we defend it. The Brits' love for their NHS is blind and unconditional. But the thing about blind, unconditional love is that it's, well, rather impersonal. It's not about the thing being loved but the feeling the person gets from loving it. As it is with the NHS. When we talk about it, we're rarely talking about our experiences with it, but merely the idea of it.

Universal healthcare for all!

The NHS is an applause term. You say how great it is, everyone claps for you. You're a good person. Your citizenship gets renewed for another year.

I don't want to criticise the idea of the NHS and the people in it who give far too much for the measly financial reward offered them. But criticising the system is not criticising the people forced to toil within it. Which leaves us in a weird paradox: everyone professes to love the NHS, few would dare criticise it, yet everyone elects to go private at the first chance.

By way of an example, some family friends lost their father in a car crash. They applied for bereavement counselling. "No problem," their friendly NHS doctor said. "I'll send in a referral, and you'll get an appointment in the post." "No problem," the friendly letter from the NHS said. "We've appointed a bereavement counsellor. Here's your appointment . . . *in six months*."

"Thanks and everything," the family said, "but we might have already done some bereaving by then. Could we possibly have an appointment a little earlier, perhaps, if it's no inconvenience and sorry for being a bother?

"No, we're underfunded. Perhaps you could consider going private?"

They went private.

If there is a condition the nation needs curing of, it's NHS myopia (I think there's a free appointment to get treatment, in nine months). NHS myopia is an inability to look past the idea of the NHS (universal healthcare is not novel anymore; there's a version of it—albeit not always as good or expansive as the NHS—in some fifty countries) in order to evaluate if, for what we're putting into it, we should be able to expect more out of it. Or, perhaps, if we should be putting more into it.

If you want to fit in, don't mention any of this hypocrisy. Just toe the national line. As soon as anyone mentions the NHS, stand up, salute, place one hand on your heart, and sing the national anthem. *The People's Glorious National Health Service?*

Wonderful.

Marvellous.

*BUT AVOID IT AT ALL COSTS.

BREXIT

I t has been suggested that we Baked Bean Enthusiasts developed our world-famous sense of humour to help reconcile falling (in just a few decades) from greatest empire the world has ever seen to, as Vladamir Putin so concisely put it, "an insignificant little island next to France".

It's a nice theory, and even if it's wrong, it suggests our humour is world renowned, which is a pleasant notion. The problem, however, is the overwhelming evidence that *we have never* accepted we're an insignificant little island next to France.

Which brings us to Brexit.

We Brits have always had a somewhat dysfunctional relationship with Europe. We were part of it, technically, but behaved as if we weren't. Like someone who has long concluded they're out of their partner's league, we held back our affections (and our currency); we were slow to answer messages; we would accidentally talk in *I* when we should have been using *we*; we snuck off and forged a "special relationship" with the USA.

Therefore, it was perhaps not such a shock, what with our inflated sense of self-importance, that at some point we'd pack our bags, declare "it's not us, *it's them,*" and dump Europe's ass.

Our breakup began with a referendum. That referendum happened because of one man: Nigel Farage. One of the best things about living in Germany is that Nigel Farage doesn't. Nigel Farage is the bore in the pub who keeps harping on about the imagined glory days of yesteryear. Everyone avoids him, unless he's buying a round. In which case they'll have a double, thanks, Nigel.

Nigel Farage is the leader of a small, loud group of carbon copies of himself. They're called the United Kingdom Independence Party (UKIP). If they were a reality TV show, they'd be called *Britain's Got Bigots*. UKIP wanted us out of Europe. They wanted the borders closed. And they wanted those things now! Irony enthusiasts might enjoy the fact that Nigel Farage's wife is German, but let's stay on topic.

UKIP polled well, for a time: 10 to 15 percent well. That's not much, you might think. However, the UK doesn't have proportional representation. So, just like the USA, in effect, we're a two-political-party country— Labour vs Conservative.

Which means your minor party is totally irrelevant unless it threatens to break the balance of power between Labour and Conservative. It just so happened that many UKIP supporters were former Conservative voters. A problem that threatened to tip 2015's general election in Labour's favour.

So Prime Minister and Supertoff™ David Cameron offered a deal. If the Conservatives were re-elected, there would be a referendum on EU membership.

It was the sort of deal that Donald Trump would

describe in a poorly punctuated late-night tweet sent from the Whitehouse bath as "an unbelievably shitty deal. Bad. Sad!" It was a political cock-block of UKIP, nothing more. But with it, Supertoff™ took what was a marginal issue, something 10 to 15 percent of the population cared about, and made it something the whole nation would be asked to inform themselves about and then vote on.

The Conservatives got re-elected. In 2016, we had that referendum. In preparation for it, two sides worked to inform/bias the nation.

The Leave Campaign

Arguably, Leave had the easier job. After all, if I stopped you in the street and asked, "Are you perfectly happy with how everything is going in your life or would you like to make some changes?" It's quite likely you'd think about it and decide, "Yeah, there are a few things I'd alter." We'd all like more control, more independence, more prosperity. The problem with Brexit is that that's pretty much where the conversation ended. The Leave campaigns (there were two main ones—Leave.eu and Vote Leave) didn't have to qualify or quantify what this word *Leave* meant. What would change. When. How.

They didn't have to show policies, projections, timeta-bles, and other such evidence of planning and rationality. The few claims they did make—most famously, "£350 million a week for the NHS"—were promptly abandoned after the result. "Our promises were a series of possibili-ties," said Leave politician Ian Duncan Smith, to the relief of anyone who has ever made a wedding vow.

As a result, the Vote Leave campaign was, as put by

one academic, "one of the most dishonest political campaigns this country [the UK] has ever seen". The Electoral Commission investigated and concluded it also broke electoral funding laws. It fined them sixty-one thousand pounds and referred two of its members to the police for prosecution.

All this came too late to change the result: that this little word, *Leave*, has come to mean a thousand different things to the people who voted for it: extra funding for the NHS; closing the borders and restricting immigration; overturning EU-set fishing quotas; sticking two fingers up to the establishment; taking back our country, whatever that means.

The Remain Campaign

Remain was about a world of fewer borders; about keeping that holiday home in Spain; about London remaining Europe's financial centre; about liberalism; about stability; about more of the same. Traditionally, referendums are won by the status quo, so Remain began with a slight advantage. But in the post-2008 financial clusterfuck, the world got a bit weird, and, like an egg in the sun, started to smell iffy. People weren't feeling stable. Didn't want more of the same.

The problems citizens faced were complex: globalisation, immigration, unfettered capitalism, machination, decaying rural communities, ageing populations fearful for their health care and pensions, years of Conservative-government austerity. Some of these issues were exacerbated by the EU, many were not. Knowing the difference involved maths, research, and separating cause from effect.

All things humans hate.

It's also proved hard to excite people about "more of the same". It's just not an engaging message. Especially when you sell it with facts. The Remain campaign liked facts. The idiots. "The remain campaign featured fact, fact, fact, fact, fact. It just doesn't work. You have got to connect with people emotionally. It's the Trump success." That's what Arron Banks, the biggest donor to the Leave campaign, told the *Guardian*. If you thought that quote was stupid but prescient, Michael Gove trumped it (see what I did there) with this now legendary sentence: "People in this country have had enough of experts."

When humans have died out and giant cockroaches rule the world, in their Natural Human Museum, there will be a special exhibit devoted to Michael Gove and this sentence. It is the klaxon of impending global doom.

The Result

Given how the two were presented, it should perhaps not have been such a surprise that when the bell rang, and the votes were counted, it was Leave that proved victorious, with 51.9 percent of the vote. It was hardly a fair fight. Leave got to mean everything to everyone. The voting slip should really have looked like this:

REFERENDUM
ON UNITED KINGDOM'S
MEMBERSHIP OF THE
EUROPEAN UNION

Assuming it was possible, and we knew how to do it, and when it would happen, and what it would mean, should we leave the European Union?

[ ] Yes   [ ] No

[ ] What was the question again? I'm so angry.
I want to do something. Is this changing something?
Change something! If possible, everything.
Burn it all down. I want my country back.

But it didn't look like this. And no matter how tight the margin (51.89 percent to 48.11 percent), it was a win for Leave. We would leave Europe. But how and when?

If the buildup to Brexit was weird, the aftermath went full *Twilight Zone*. Supertoff™ resigned and *Game of I-don't-want-the Throne* began. The people who had pushed for Brexit (Boris Johnson, in particular) and would have been logical choices to run the Conservative Party rushed to abdicate faster than everyone else in what looked from the outside like the world's politest game of musical chairs:

"Sit, please. I insist."

"No, after you."

"Me? I enjoy standing."

It's easy to simplify Brexit, to make it a battle of left vs right, city vs rural, educated vs uneducated, nationalists vs internationalists, young vs old. But it isn't simple. The EU is nuanced. Messy. Complicated. If any Brits were absolutely certain which way to vote in the referendum, I'd say they were delusional. That they'd failed to understand the complexity of the issue. Multiculturalism doesn't advantage us all equally. If you aren't pro-Europe, you aren't automatically a right-wing, closed-minded, xenophobic bigot.

Was the referendum fair?

Absolutely not.

Could the EU be better?

No doubt.

Is it in need of reform?

Sure.

Just as everything more complicated than the local choir could be improved and reformed. In the EU's defence, how could the politics, laws, governance, and resource allocation of twenty-eight nations, comprising some seven hundred million people, not be massively complicated? Unfathomably complex? How could it possibly function without colossal wastage, corruption, lobbying, compromise, entrenched bureaucracy, and abnormal-banana-curvature laws?

Bananas aside, it couldn't. But that doesn't mean we should scrap it, nor blindly accept it as good. Personally, I believe the problems we face now—climate change, resource shortages, nuclear weapon proliferation, technological unemployment—are bigger than two hundred mini-fiefdoms can solve. However, I'm open to being wrong on that. Perhaps the EU will collapse. Perhaps aliens will arrive and obliterate us all. Perhaps Brexit will be a smart economic move in the long run. We just can't know that yet. After all, broken watches are correct twice a day.

Article 50 has been filed. We have left the European Union. Six years after that fateful vote of summer 2016, in a year where many greats died (David Bowie, Prince, Muhammad Ali), it's still too early to know if we've something else to add to that list: Great Britain.

PEOPLE LIKE US VS PEOPLE
LIKE THEM

I n 1941, George Orwell said Britain was "the most
class-ridden society under the sun".

In 1941, he was probably right, if we ignore the
sun part. In 1941, we were almost certainly the most class-
ridden society under patchy rain clouds. But back then,
you could get socially ostracised for drinking the wrong
brand of tea, pronouncing "scone" incorrectly (upper-class
people say "scoan", the great unwashed favour a "sgone"),
or having too few (or many) servants. Even our boozers,
the places where we were supposed to meet and mingle,
where all people are equal, were split (voluntarily) into
"public" (for the lower classes) and "saloon" (for middle
and upper). Parliament was (mostly still is) an Us vs Them
affair with the House of Lords (Them) and the House of
Commons (Us).

In short, class was everything. But then the Second
World War broke down these divisions and thrust women
into work. Prosperous post-war Britain offered unparal-
leled opportunities for social mobility, free of the old rules
and conventions. Throw in the transition from rural to city,

from factory to office, globalisation, immigration, the EU. It became less important what university your father studied at or what your last name was.

We were just John, Simon, Gemma, and Joan now.

The two sides of the pub mixed. We all became servants of multiculturalism and liberalism.

As a result, today, British society has taken on the shape of a middle-aged man—thin at the top and lumpy around the middle.

However, none of this means we Brits have stopped caring about class. Old habits die hard, especially fun habits like being judgemental about people you don't know. So, while many of our old rivalries have died, our enjoyment of those rivalries lives on. We remain bloodhounds sniffing out signs that we're in the presence of a class interloper, a fake, a fraud. Someone pretending to be one of us when really, she's not. Someone who secretly went to boarding school. Someone putting on a cockney accent when he grew up in Coventry. Someone who would change the channel from football to cricket if she thought no one was looking. We're always scanning for class. Listening to accents. Looking at how people hold their knife and fork (the tines of the fork curved inward, towards you, is lower; outward, away from you, is upper) and whether they call the room that contains the toilet the "lavatory", "loo", "toilet", or "bog".

Not that we're against "poshing up" or "slumming down" ourselves, though. It feels nicer to fit in than to stand out. So, it's logical we'd take the path of least resistance and adopt the local dialect while trash-talking with the other dads at football on Saturday morning, and then perfectly articulate our *th*s over dinner with the in-laws, and then be all "nah mate" and "innit" in Wetherspoons later that night with the gang from work. The next

47

morning, hungover, we bow and "namaste" our guru at yoga.

We just won't admit we're doing this. In Britain, class has become little more than a big game of People Like Us vs People Like Them. With everyone swapping jerseys to fit in, depending on the situation they find themselves in and the norms of the People Like Us group they want to belong to.

"All societies," Australian scholar George Watson once said, "are unequal . . . but they describe their own inequalities variously." In that case, I'd say that even if they don't matter much anymore, we Brits like to describe them—really, really often.

MEET THE CLASSES

I'll now briefly summarise the three main social classes in the UK according to stereotypes, thereby ensuring I'll lose friends in all of them.

The Lower-Class Leftovers (aka Chavs, Prolls, the Underclasses, the Great Unwashed, Commoners, Kappa Slappers, Townies, Pikeys, Neds, Hoodies, Yobs, Free School Meal-ers)

We've already talked about the difficulty of trying to live up to the Ideal of Britishness. What's interesting about the lowest class is that either they've never learned of these expectations or they've simply given up trying to adhere to them. Which should make them the freest people in British society. However, their brazenness and willingness to stand out makes them an easy figure of ridicule, which makes them care even less about fitting in, which makes them more identifiable and thus easier figures of ridicule.

Many people wrongly assume this social group doesn't have values. It does—they're just different values; not traditional education but "street smarts", not working hard but "hustling". How can you spot these underlings? You don't need to find them. They'll find you. They're the ones using their mobile phone as a speaker on the back of the bus, or taking selfies in Nando's, or swearing at you for getting in their way at the mall. Like Pac-Man, the other social classes will be constantly vigilant as they move around the maze of their everyday, trying not to get cornered by these Ghosts of Opportunities Past.

What they like: Bling, sportswear, white trainers, generously applied fake tan, football, gold jewellery, payday loans, binge drinking, pimped cars, profanity (especially the C-word), regional dialects, tattoos.
What they don't like: Rules, authority, people "staring at them", punctuation.,!
Values: Hedonism, alcoholism, dog-eat-dog-ism, Greggsism.
Most likely to say: "*Wot* u lookin' at, u c***?"
Least likely to say: "Am I proud of being a muggah? *Nah mate*. But 'r we not all just rational actors working within an unfair economic system? Don't think of it as theft or robbery, like. It's really more an understandable act

of capital err . . . *redistribution*, innit? Yeah. I thank you wholeheartedly for your contribution to my class struggle, middle-class comrade."

The Middle-Class Masses (aka the Radio 4 Set, Petty Bourgeoisie, Helicopter Parents)

The problem with identifying with the middle class is that 7/10 people identify as it. There's safety in numbers, after all, and while you're not winning, you're not losing either.

Middle-class problems are the problems of catchment areas, fitting holidays around term times, and arguments over who is going to pick up Zacharia from his piano lesson. Ninety-four percent of the classes' children are gluten intolerant. The middle classes may still speak in a local dialect, but many will have deliberately lost theirs. Whether they went to university or not, all middle-class parents will aspire to see their children to go. With the luxury of more time, the middle classes are likely to care about politics and be involved in their communities. With something to lose, and a reasonable chance of losing it, they peer precariously over their shoulders, looking for signs they're falling behind.

What they like: Gastropubs, Wimbledon, Spanish holidays, Radio 4, theatre, asserting excessive influence over every tiny detail of the development of their children, inspirational-quote wall art about dancing like no one is watching.

What they don't like: Anything they perceive as threatening their (often idealised and mythical) British values.

Values: Family first, doing what's right.

Most likely to say: "I'm just going to nip quickly into Waitrose to get some hummus and a bottle of Grigio before *Bake Off* starts."

Least likely to say: "No, I'm not too worried about the GCSE results of the local comprehensive. I'm sure they're doing the best job they can. I mean, really, people make such a fuss about schools. Not every child can be the brain of Britain. It's fine that our Sarah is one of the slower children in her grade. I'm sure she'll make a very personable stripper one day."

The Upper-Class Elites (aka Toffs, Hoorah Henrys, Yar Yars, the Oxbridge Set, Yuppies, the Hoi Polloi)

Since so few truly-upper-class people exist, and almost all of them live in the posher enclaves of the home counties, in dwellings with large, intimidating electric gates, very little is known about this elusive social group. They're cultural unicorns. As a result, they are little more than a shallow stereotype or vague threat depicted sitting in their country home, in a wax jacket, eating pheasant, near a photo of themselves with Prince Charles. On the coffee table is the draft of a new legislation designed to shaft the poor out of their last potato.

Actual upper classers might be exactly like this caricature, or might not, as is their choosing. They can be whatever they want because they have time, money, contacts, and generations of impeccable breeding behind them.

They have won. Class is largely irrelevant to them. Still, they are likely to identify as part of "the Oxbridge set" (meaning they've studied at Cambridge or Oxford). This class won't just own a home—they will own "land". And by own, I mean inherit. If they're lucky, they might also inherit a nice fancy title: duke, earl, viscount, or something of that ilk. If not, they might have to make do with just a jaw-busting double- or triple-barrelled surname such as Heathcote-Tempest-Wilks, Vane-Tempest-Dorrien, or a mediocre Cunningham-Blakeley.

What they like: Hunting, polo, nannies, homeopathy, ostentatiousness, four-by-fours, horses, members' clubs, opera, ballet, rubbing hundred-pound notes on themselves and cackling.

What they don't like: Taxation, class interbreeding, immigration.

Values: Education, peerage, conservatism.

Most likely to say: "Oh you live there, do you, darling? How delightfully ethnic"; "We have a bread-maker, too! Her name's Ausra"; and, "Yes, well, people these days want everything given to them on a silver platter, that's the problem."

Least likely to say: "Everything I have has been given to me on a silver platter—that's my problem."

16

HOMEOWNERS FC VS RENTERS UNITED

T here is one class division that matters enormously. A divide that has split the whole country into two teams: Homeowners FC vs Renters United.

To understand the intense rivalry between the two sides, you need to understand the baffling world of British real estate—in which the average house price rose from around £150,000 in 2005 to £217,000 in July 2016, while wages remained stagnant.

Because of this, Home Owners FC has become a bit of a bully; a Bayern Munich, Barcelona, or Manchester

United getting ever better and richer. Renters United, on the other hand, is the local amateur team made up of the lost, the damned, the financially precarious, the students, and someone's Yorkshire terrier. They're trained by Mick, a guy someone met down at the pub, who, while possessing no formal qualifications, has always felt that he knows a thing or two about the beautiful game.

Not things he's been able to express yet, bless him. This team is not doing so well.

Following the progress of your team is a national obsession. Everyone passes their evenings on Rightmove.co.uk, basking in the glow of their tablets, checking the latest score. If you belong to Homeowners FC, you cheer when your home goes up in value, even though everyone else's has as well. Renters United team members look on aghast, watching their dreams slip away as house-price inflation increases faster than they can scrape together a deposit so they can swap sides. A swap that would finally give them the security of not being turfed from their rented home with just a month's notice, or getting another letter saying their rent is going up, again.

We don't do renting like civilised countries, with a fair balance of rights between the two teams involved, and where homes are considered a right, not a magic cash cow endlessly milked by the middle and upper classes.

Everyone's aware the match is rigged, that Homeowners FC is too strong, that we should change the rules, but somehow those rules never get changed. Perhaps because the people with the power to do so tend to be part of team Homeowners FC and so are doing just fine. And, anyway, Bank of Mum and Dad, like Russian oligarchs in the Premier League, keep the market afloat with regular cash injections to their progeny. So the match continues and the nation cheers and laments along with it.

The Property Ladder

17

I'M A CITIZEN—GET ME OUT OF HERE

A friend of Annett's tells a story about her first week studying in London. She's taking a walk with a friend, it's a nice late-summer's evening, and they stop to buy a beer from a corner shop. They take a few sips while strolling across a bridge. They like this London thing. It's very pleasant.

When they reach the other side of the bridge, a police car skids up in front of them, blocking them on the pavement. Two police officers jump out, take the beer from them, and pour it down the nearest drain, before (lightly) fining them for public drinking.

She laughs as she tells the story. "I didn't care about the beer or the fine—it was just the speed with which it happened. We couldn't work out how someone could possibly have seen us that quickly, alerted the police, found some with nothing more important to do with their time, and then had them drive over to us. In less than two minutes."

I know how: CCTV.

We're not only obsessive about monitoring our place

on the property ladder, we're also passionate about monitoring each other. If you say the UK is a nanny state, people usually think you're talking about Mary Poppins. Our modern-day Poppins is the Government Communication Headquarters (GCHQ). Our version of the NSA. Having deduced that a spoonful of surveillance helps "terrorism" go down, they've been heaping great mountains of it on our society for the past decades. As a result, we've the dubious honour of being the most watched people on earth. It's the world's biggest reality TV show, where sixty-five million people play Truman, "good afternoon, good evening, and good night-ing" to 1.85 million cameras each day. One for every thirty-five citizens. For a progressive country, we have some of the most bizarre, overreaching security and surveillance systems on earth. Britain is the country that trust forgot.

We've an Investigatory Powers Act (deemed illegal by the European Court of Justice) that records the metadata from every phone call and all our Internet searches for a year. Internet searches that are already restricted by what's commonly known as the Great Firewall of Britain. Speaking of dubious honours: Reporters Without Borders listed us with China, Iran, Pakistan, Russia, and Saudi Arabia on a list of "Enemies of the Internet". *Enemy* is a strong word. We'd probably go with something softer —*unfriend*, perhaps.

This is probably why we Brits are such avid reality TV viewers. With no expectation of privacy in our personal lives, we've no problem watching other people lose theirs either. And at least they get to do so for the chance of a cash prize.

It's surprising how quickly you get used to the feeling of being watched. By now, when I have a great punchline, or snappy retort, I like to check I'm in the centre frame of the nearest CCTV camera. You never know who might be watching. I don't want to get evicted this week. I like to imagine operatives at GCHQ munching on popcorn and making Best of Adam 2018 highlights reels. We get to practice for our debut on *Britain's Got Talent* or *Big Brother* through our daily cameos on GCHQ's *Britain's Got Terrorists*.

Warning!

This nation is under twenty-four-hour CCTV surveillance.

CHAPTER 3

"Actions speak louder than words"

How We Interact with Each Other

Ministry of CIVIL OBEDIENCE

A request for refrain.

Dear Citizens,

Please restrain from displays of emotive exuberance. Emotions are like genitals: best kept hidden until after a few drinks.

Your fellow Underground users appreciate your polite refrain and measured indifference.

Yours sincerely,

BRITAIN.

1 8

SOCIAL SOFTENERS

My girlfriend tells a story about a group tour holiday in Sri Lanka, where she was the token German amongst a dozen Brits. The group was scheduled to play cricket in a local village. They group didn't want to play cricket because . . . *cricket*. So one of the girls volunteered to send the tour guide a message to get them out of it.

"Oh my god, this message," Julia said, pinching her forehead. "It was the length of *War and Peace*. But just full of peace. Oh, and about a dozen *sorries*. The actual request was in there, somewhere, but it was like she went looking for a haystack of niceties to hide it in."

For the next part she adopts a mock English accent:

"Hi, Mark. How are you? Good, I hope. Today was great, thanks again. We all really enjoyed it and we're excited for tomorrow. If it's no problem for you, and sorry for the late notice, and again, no problem if not, but we were perhaps possibly wondering if there might be any way we could potentially not do the cricket activity tomorrow? Again, only

*if it's no bother at all. Sorry for the inconvenience. Have a
nice evening."*

I laugh a knowing laugh: *social softeners.* Social softeners
are like bubble wrap for requests, blankets for requisitions,
padding for petitions, and lubricant for inquiries. Like the
softener you use when doing laundry, social softeners help
to keep our interactions light, fluffy, and cuddly. They also
let the person we're asking something from know that he or
she has the right to decline a request without it turning into
a con*back*tation that never ends until one party moves away
to escape his or her demons.

My nation-folk tend to label all foreigners as rude. The
reason for this, I think, is merely that other cultures don't
require social softeners. In those places, people are
permitted to come out and say what they want. To
exchange facts without first exchanging pleasantries. But
we Brits are delicate, sensitive flowers, prone to wilt if not
handled gently. So, if it's no inconvenience, and while
we're sorry to ask, and it's no problem if you can't, but we
were wondering, and we're sorry to be a bother, but could
you perhaps possibly consider adding social softeners when
you talk to us? Thanks . . .

BANTER

B ecause British culture is relentlessly polite—we'll thank cars that stop at zebra crossings even though they were legally required to; we'll hold a door open *until* there's someone to hold it open for, even if that takes a full minute—we'll treat a friend we bump into outside the supermarket just as warmly as we'll treat a mortal enemy. So how do people know which they are?

Simple. With your friends, you banter.

Banter is showing a person how much you like him by talking to him as if you hate him. It's the adult equivalent of the boy in the playground teasing the girl he fancies. Genius, right? What could go wrong?

To do it: divorce *the content* of what you're saying from *the meaning* transmitted with it. The more warmth you feel for the person you're bantering with, the larger the division should be. Here's an example conversation.

What we say/banter	What we feel
Friend 1: "Oh, you again. Like I haven't seen enough of your ugly mug lately."	Friend 1: I'm crazy about you. You push all my buttons. You're my best friend in the whole world.
Friend 2: "Your mum seemed happy to see it last night when I got into her bed!"	Friend 2: When I look at you ... I mean ... this is going to sound silly, but ... I just ... feel ... there's this warmth in my chest.
Friend 1: "Ouch. Nice one. Well, her eyes aren't what they used to be, bless her. She probably confused you with an actual man."	Friend 1: Sometimes it just feels a bit too—
Friend 2: "Yeah, probably. Must have been disappointing for her, although I guess with you as a son she's no stranger to disappointment. *Waiter!* Your round or mine?"	Friend 2: —stop. I know. I know. Me too.

Because we're uncomfortable showing emotions in a positive way, we've developed this weird system that allows us to show them in a (fake) negative way. Because of the Law of Banter, when Annett and I started dating I would tease her, all day, every day. I think this confused her in the beginning because she would say things like, "Stop that!", "Why are you being mean?", and "I thought you liked me?"

Looking back, it was probably a difficult time for her. But I persevered. I had to show her how I felt—by making her think I felt the exact opposite. It would all be worth it in the end. Probably.

It took some time to convince her of it. I forget exactly how long. Five or six years, perhaps. But eventually she did begin to enjoy this bantering thing. It was a new conversational function. She had permission to say horrible things to another human without it ending in a duel. We could also show off how strong our relationship had become by taking turns to set it on fire with our words.

Not that this meant she was good at it. It's a difficult skill to get right. Many times, she thought she was bantering, believed what she was saying was playfully offensive, when it was actually just really, really hurtful. What followed was a quite difficult adjustment period for me. It took some time. I forget exactly how much. Five or six years, perhaps. I'd let a genie out of the lamp. It was not my place to ask it to go back in again. Eventually, like Goldilocks, we got it *just right*.

So, banter with us as if your life depended on it—and it does. Well, your social life, anyway.

THREE STRIKES AND
THEY'RE OUT

It's morning, I'm in the kitchen of my parents' house toasting crumpets.* My mum hovers near me. I can tell from the look on her face that she has something she wants to say—she's wearing her Mask of Civility quite poorly, perhaps because it's morning. She busies herself wiping the counter-top. A surface she wipes every fifteen minutes. Nothing on earth is more thoroughly wiped.

She exhales.

"Something you want to say?" I ask, looking up from my glass of orange juice.

"No," she says. "Everything's fine."

Fine. The least fine word in the English language.

She wants to tell me something, but not yet. Because in our culture, it's illegal to reveal your feelings before you've been asked for them at least three times.

Three strikes and they're out, I call it. It's like baseball, but for emotions. Violating it gets you sent to oversharing prison. Where you're forced to bunk with people who constantly require emotional support.

Yuck.

In some cultures, like my adopted Germany, people are permitted to be honest with each other. We Brits are liars. Sweet liars. Kind liars. More likely to fib for your benefit than our own; to avoid awkwardness; to keep things harmonious.

But liars nonetheless.

We'll tell you that you look nice in that dress, when really you look like a run-over hippo. We'll tell you your signature peach pie tastes good, when it has all the flavour of warm gravel. We'll tell you it was lovely to meet you, when we've already forgotten your name. We can't always be trusted with our words. Which is why we must hold back the important ones. Build tension. Let you know that what we're about to say, when we do finally reveal it to you, well, it means something.

Back to the kitchen. "I'm pretty sure there is?" I say.

Strike two.

"No," she says, unconvincingly, having paused for just a second too long. "It's fine."

"Sure . . . ?"

Third strike.

She tuts. "Well . . ." She pauses her half-hearted wiping. "Your sister is annoyed with you."

"Okay," I say, surprised, since I'm an exemplary sibling. "What's she annoyed about?"

"That you didn't go and see your nieces yesterday."

I frown. "Is she going to tell me that herself?"

"No, I don't think so. I'm also not supposed to have told you, so don't tell her I did. Okay?"

I take another sip of juice. "So, just to clarify, she's annoyed with me, but I can't tell her I know that, because that would reveal to her that you've told me that she's annoyed with me, which you're not allowed to do, but have done, right?"

She nods. "Right."

"So, you've just dumped this on me. I now have to pretend everything is okay, when it isn't, while being extra nice, to make up for the thing that she says, to you, that I've done wrong, even though I don't agree that it was wrong?"

"Right." She confirms as if this makes perfect sense, is just another Saturday.

This can't be the functioning of a normal society. I want to tell her what I really think about it, but she doesn't ask me enough times, so I can't. I swallow my annoyance down. The con*back*tation between my sister and me will continue. I eat my crumpets and vow to be extra nice to her and extra enthusiastic about her offspring. These people might be crazy, but they're still my people.

*Impossibly delicious, soft breakfast yeast sponges that live at the intersection of crunch, crumble, and perfection.

21

MONOLINGUALISM

I t's my personal belief that the British Empire was the most extravagant attempt the world has ever seen to ensure a civilisation would never again have to learn a foreign language. It wasn't saffron and gold that we wanted—it was *Zafferano* and *Oro* that we didn't.

If you think that's ridiculous, what's truly absurd is that we pretty much succeeded. South American mountain villages can be a bit tricky, sure, but otherwise we're well on our way to total global English-language dominance. Why start with German or Esperanto or Mandarin now? Everyone will speak English soon enough. Just wait it out.

We're waiting it out, in case you haven't noticed.

We might pretend otherwise. Might let the occasional "*Zwei bier, bitte*", "*Parlez-vous Innglish?*", or "*Grassy-ass, senor!*" slip out, but don't believe it. We've retired from the language-learning game. A game we don't know the rules of and have never played. We're stubbornly monolingual. The British are into foreign languages in much the same way squirrels are into yachting.

In my high school, this charade was particularly obvious. The curriculum reserved a paltry two hours and twenty minutes for foreign languages a week. Just one language was offered: French. The language of the country we despise more than any other. If that wasn't enough of a hint about how our curriculum viewed all the world's languages not our own, the French teacher assigned to us was Irish. She brought a wonderful but largely incomprehensible lilt to the language of romance. Unfortunately, none of us learned enough to judge if she was qualified to teach it, perhaps its own damning conclusion. After seven years of treating the class as an extension of playtime, we finished where we began—*Livre un*, *mi amour*.

Of course, we're aware there are small children in Belgium who can talk about the weather in six languages. But they're not us. And the weather in Belgium is probably not as complex as it is here. And, anyway, they're obviously running some kind of superior, foreign mental hardware. If we can accept the idea that Dutch people are tall, that Russians write great literature, and that the French are wonderful shruggers, could it not also be possible that Brits simply cannot speak foreign languages? That our carbohydrate-pummelled heads can't contain more than one word for *carbohydrate*? That with each exotic new foreign word that goes in, another must be let out? What if that word is something important? A *sorry*, *take care*, or *blimey*?

It's just better not to risk it. To stay monolingual. Which is why when you talk to us, we won't be meeting in the middle—we'll be meeting in English.

Sorry about that.

22

"RIGHT THEN . . ."

As any good director knows, transitions matter. You can't just jump sharply from one scene to the next. The small in-between moments, the transitions from where we are to where we're going next—they're the glue that's holding the whole story together, that tugs the audience along with the narrative.

As it is in art, it is in life: transitions matter. If we get them wrong, the people around us will be left bewildered and unable to follow. For example, imagine you're sitting in a restaurant. You've eaten. You've paid the bill. It's time to leave.

You want to stand up.

But you're sitting down.

Everyone knows you as someone sitting down.

They understand Sitting Down You.

Will they comprehend new Upright You?!?! Dynamic, mobile, full of thrust, whim, and purpose?

They might find that new you confusing, jarring, untrustworthy. Perhaps they'll be able to follow your developing narrative. You were down, you are now up. It's not exactly quantum entanglement, but still, wouldn't it be nicer to warn those in your vicinity first?

It would, and accordingly, we Brits have devised an ingenious solution for just these situations. It's the phrase "right then . . ."

Think of it as an early-transition-warning system.

To get up from a table without saying it is, for us, unthinkable. In fact, doing anything we are not currently doing without first saying it is similarly incomprehensible. We would be incoherent. Jarring. Erratic. Loose social cannons. Etiquette renegades.

Using it is simple: directly before you're about to transition, take a theatrically sharp intake of breath, ideally lasting at least five seconds (pretend your head is a child's helium balloon that needs inflating). Next, say, "Right the*nnnn*." Fade slowly out on the *n* using the remainder of that bonus breath.

A transition is about to occur. Everyone understands. Everyone can follow. Order is maintained. There is no situation or action that cannot be improved with the addition of a sturdy, buttressing "right then".

All else is jump-cut anarchy.

23

FIGHT PRAISE

The British treat praise as *Mission Impossible* briefings that must be discarded before they self-destruct. Perhaps you've tried to compliment one of us, only to be given the compliment back, as if you'd presented us not with a few nice words about a lasagne recipe but something wholly inappropriate, like a solid gold pony worth five million pounds?

"It's just a little something I've thrown together. Jamie Oliver did all the hard work."

"This old thing? I've had it ages."

"We all get lucky sometimes."

"Oh, it was nothing . . ."

We're required to have an almost pathological modesty. I was reminded of this recently when playing five-a-side football with my English friend Paul, who had played so well it was as if the ball had been stuck to his foot and detached itself only to fly into hard-to-reach corners of the goal.

He used every possible method to deflect my compliments.

"You had a great game," I said to him after, as we waited for the tram home. He shifted his gaze to the ground. His skin took on the hue of a tomato. "I was shit last week," he replied, as if this was of any relevance to the compliment I'd just given him.

"*Okay* . . . but you were great this week."

"No. You were great, I thought." (Compliment Switcheroo: in which you attempt to deflect the compliment back onto the other person, regardless of whether it fits.)

"I played the game like I'd just this minute discovered it. I fell over five times. I missed an open goal. How many goals did you score? Ten?"

"Did I?" (Redundant Question: a good delaying tactic)

"You did," I confirmed, keeping him pinned against the compliment mat.

"Oh," he replied, with a hint of resentment. "This tram is always late. And busy. Annoying, right?" (Topic Change and Opinion as Question: a dazzling combo!)

"You're great at avoiding compliments," I said. (Compliment about Being Uncomplimentable? There's nothing in the playbook for this.)

He had no response. He went cross-eyed as he stared up at the clouds.

"Weather forecast for tomorrow is good," he said.

24

FINETHANKSANDYOU?

There's one social softener that's so important it needs its own entry. Do you know the most-asked question in the UK? No, it's not, "Cuppa?" (although that runs close). Live amongst us, briefly visit us, it makes no difference—you'll still be asked this question a dozen times a day. If you pricked us, we'd bleed it.

The question is: "How are you?"

It's a simple little question, yet many foreigners get the answer wrong. Germans, especially. Because they've been raised on a strict diet of truth and honesty, they want to answer something like this:

"*Schlecht*. I have this problem with my back. It's affecting my sleep. I was at the doctor's, but he wasn't helping me. Doctors, you know? I googled it, and it's possible I've been bitten by a poisonous Peruvian tree frog. I have all the symptoms anyway."

Wrong answer, pal.

There is only one acceptable response to the question "How are you?" That answer is "Finethanksandyou?" (must be spoken as one word).

It doesn't matter who asks. Doesn't matter if you've been run over by a monster truck, are bleeding out on the pavement, and can feel the cold, bony finger of the Reaper upon your shoulder. When the paramedic appears and asks you how you are, and she will ask, you answer, "Finethanksandyou?"

It might seem like our hourly—*how are you, I'm fine, how are you, I'm fine*—small-talk performances are completely pointless. That's not the case. It's just that in this dance, as is our specialty, the meaning is in the subtext and sentiment, not in the words leaving our lips.

What is said	What is communicated
Person A: "Hi. How are you?"	Person A: *You still exist! Great!*
Person B: "Finethanksandyou?"	Person B: *I still exist. So do you! Great!*
Person A: "Yeah, fine, thanks."	Person A: *We're mortal. One day, all this, all this us, will be over. Can you believe that? It's just going to end. This is it, this is all there is.*
Person B: "Weather is supposed to be nice this weekend. Anyway, take care!"	Person B: *I know, friend. I fear it too . . .*
Person A: "You too."	Person A: *Let's hope it's a long way off yet. Be well, buddy.*

My dad had a colleague who would answer the question "How are you?" with just the simple, short, abrupt "Yeah, you?" Everyone made fun of her (behind her back, of course). Her nickname became Yeah, You. I have a certain respect for her. She had obviously seen through the whole ruse of this question and therefore created an answer that was optimised, condensed, and efficient.

Yeah, you?

THE IMPOLITENESS PURGE

I 've made it clear that in Paddington Bear Land, we're ineffably polite. I've spent less time on the why. It's not because of our good nature, sense of common decency, or desire to avoid scenes.

It's because of The Impoliteness Purge (TIP).

TIP is a daily nationwide competition we're all forced to take part in. A simple, sinister competition with high stakes. Every time you say "please" or "thank you", you earn a point. At the end of each day, the ten people in the country with the fewest points are deported to France.

Yeah, I said the stakes were high.

For a British person, there's nothing more terrifying than the prospect of exile in France; no one speaks a bloody word of English; there's blood in the meat; they eat snails; everyone's better looking than you; seven times as cultured; and yet you're still so close to home you can gaze lovingly at the white cliffs of Dover. At a land where people make sense and don't keep striking all the damn time.

I spent many months explaining TIP to Annett, preparing her for trips to visit my family. Letting her know that P's and Q's are serious business in these (rainy) parts. Unfortunately, she had a erman gruffness that proved hard to shift. She showed no aptitude for excessive politeness.

I remember a trip to Marks & Spencer where she was buying a pair of trousers. The process of buying something is an excellent opportunity to quickly amass TIP points. We can squeeze seven thank yous into the purchase of a pack of chewing gum. The cashier will join in too, of course. He'll have his TIP score to worry about. This trouser purchase was the perfect moment for Annett to put everything I'd taught her into practice. I stood observing at the side of the till, noting her progress on a clipboard I'd brought for just such an occasion.

It did not go well.

"I'm getting better at this, you know?" she said, coming over with her bag in hand, the trousers purchased.

"Seriously?" I said. "You think that went well?"

"I said 'thank you' three times."

I looked down at my clipboard. "It was twice."

"Twice as much as normal. And I got one 'please' in."

I tutted. She deserved it.

"Ouch. Don't tut me. What was wrong?"

"Did you not notice my squirming?"

"No."

"There were, conservatively, at least six further opportunities to say 'please' or 'thank you' during that exchange. It went so badly I couldn't even watch by the end. You were unbelievably rude."

"Really? But I thought I was very polite."

"You were many things, Annett, but not *polite*. We can never come here again. Assuming they'd let us, anyway. Sometimes I wonder if you're scared of France at all. Hand me one of those reduced men's ties, I'm going to hang myself."

PLEASE AND THANK YOU—THE RETAIL EDITION

Should you find yourself visiting us and in need of trousers, here's a breakdown of how to behave in a way that will help you amass a high TIP score and meet the elevated politeness expectations of my people.

Retail Transaction Step	Expected Behaviour Abroad	Expected Behaviour in the UK
Put the item(s) down on the counter.	Stare directly ahead. Do not blink. It's a sign of weakness.	Smile. Nod. Say, "Thank you" earnestly, as if the person has done you a tremendous favour, such as donating you a kidney. Her last kidney.
Cashier takes the items.	Stare directly ahead. Do not blink.	Say, "Thank you." Smile 27 percent more enthusiastically.
Cashier asks if you would like a bag.	Shake your head briskly.	Say, "Yes, please. Thank you. Please. If it's no bother. Thank you. Thanks."
Cashier puts the items in a bag.	Stare directly ahead. Do not blink.	Say, "Thank you."
Cashier tells you the final amount.	Act as if the amount is ten times what's fair, right, and reasonable. Stare the swindler of a cashier down. Do not blink.	Say, "Thank you," as if the amount is so low she's practically paying you to take the items away.
Hand your card to the cashier.	Stare directly ahead. Do not blink.	Say, "Thank you."
Cashier returns your card and receipt.	Stare directly ahead. Do not blink.	Say, "Thank you. Thanks. Cheers. Nice. Wow. Thanks. Please." Act as if you were never expecting to get the card back and its return is a wonderful surprise.
Take the bag, turn around, and leave.	Say, "Thanks," but as if you're using the word for the first time and unsure how it works. If feeling particularly chipper, consider an additional "Bye" or "See ya" (optional, discouraged).	Say, "Thank you." Turn around. Say, "See you." Bow. Wave. Smile. Walk backwards, curtsying until you reach the exit. Shout "Thank you" one last time, for luck.

WHAT WE'RE TALKING ABOUT
WHEN WE'RE TALKING ABOUT
THE WEATHER

The British are, broadly speaking, small-talk monogamous. When we slip between social sheets we like to find the same faithful conversation partners waiting, none more than our old flame: The Weather. Stereotypes are almost always based on some kernel of truth, albeit distorted and amplified for comedic effect. The Brits' meteorological obsession is not exaggerated. Underestimated, even. We generate atmosphere amongst us by talking about the atmosphere above us. We discuss it with the sort of passion and zeal that would make you think we're trading insider secrets, or gossiping about the love lives of the neighbours, not merely sharing information anyone can get by looking through the nearest pane of glass. Information about something we can't even influence. Information about something that's always a disappointment anyway.

So, why do we keep doing it?

As already discussed, Britain used to be a class-stratified society. We're certainly still class conscious. In our daily lives—watching our children play in the park, waiting in line at the cafeteria, greeting a fellow dog walker we've always thought is kind of shifty looking—we often find ourselves propelled into conversation with strangers. Strangers whose lives we know nothing beyond what we can sleuth from their clothing, dialect, and manners. We need to quickly find common ground.

What do we have in common? The weather.

The weather is the single most harmless, inoffensive, unprovocative, unpolitical topic going. Under the weather we're all united. It's the vanilla of small talk. The cucumber of discourse. A lifeboat in a stormy sea of (real and imagined) class difference. Because even Her Majesty —with all her corgis, servants, tax money, and jewel-encrusted hats, rattling around in her palaces and stately homes—still gets wet when we get wet. Is still cold when we're cold. Looks out the window and wishes, just as we plebs do, that the British summer lasted longer than twelve minutes in late August.So, we talk about the weather. And you should, too. With us. Which reminds me, I hear it's supposed to be a nice weekend? Lot of rain lately, right? I wouldn't mind a little of that global warming they keep banging on about . . .

CHAPTER 4

"All mouth and no trousers"

Our Language and Humour

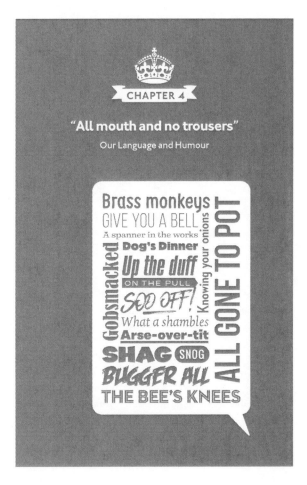

(BADLY) RECEIVED
PRONUNCIATION

There's something called received pronunciation (RP). It's the English that the Queen and our political class speak. Margaret Thatcher took elocution lessons just to be able to express all the awful things she wanted to do to our society in RP. Almost no one speaks it. It's like the Atlantis of British accents.

However, thanks to the BBC World Service, Hugh Grant romcoms, study-English CDs, and Monty Python, it has become the default accent deluded foreign types expect us to have.

Then they come and visit us...

They're confident about the trip. They've had English class for years at school, after all. They consider Stephen Fry a lovable honorary uncle. They've read all the Harry Potters—twice. They know eight words of cockney rhyming slang. They've spent one hundred hours perfecting their *th*s. They're ready to show off their language skills.

Then they get off a plane, get on a train, get off that train, and get into a taxi. There, they meet a real-life

English person. That person's mouth moves, and words come out of it. Incomprehensible words. They *freeze*.

Was that English? It didn't sound like English. They look around. A red double-decker bus drives past. Sitting in it is a man eating a sandwich. Light rain tip-taps against the taxi window.

They are in England. It must have been the English language. "Sorry . . . ?" they stammer.

The man makes those weird mouth sounds again. They guess at what he wants. It's probably just him, they think. They'll understand everyone else just fine.

But then it keeps happening. No matter where they go or whom they interact with—the nice waitress in the restaurant, the ticket seller at the museum, the moustachioed man behind the bar. Gibberish, all of it. They start wondering what they've been taught all those years. They start doubting themselves.

They shouldn't. It's not them, it's us.

The average Brit speaks English as if she's talking through a muddy shoe. We take pride in speaking a bastard gutter-ghetto English, a messy swamp of slang and idioms and sticky swear words and lazy, lumpy pronunciation. Nouns end at the midway point. Glottal stops turn water into *wolltah*. Words change meaning. In Liverpool, *la* is a friend; everywhere else it's a musical note. In the Midlands, *mash* is something you can do to tea, not just potatoes. In London, Apples and pears mean stairs?! We've a new and equally incomprehensible dialect every seven miles. We use miles. I mean, come on! It's chaos.

It's only when I moved to Germany that I realised how bad I was at the only language I knew how to speak. It was quite a shock. I was one of only two native English speakers in the company, so other departments would send me English texts for correction. That lasted two weeks, until they noticed I had no idea how the English language worked. I sent their creations back with more mistakes than when I'd received them. They began sending the texts to the Scandinavian team instead. They spoke such lovely English, after all.

Orally, I was no better. I'd go up to a colleague to ask for something and we'd have a whole conversation in which he'd nod and smile and answer in a way that I thought was context appropriate. Then when I turned to leave, he'd say something like, "Adam, what we just talked about here, can you write it all in an e-mail?"

And I'd know. I'd see it in his eyes. He'd not followed a word of what I'd said. Even though he could speak flawless English. Just the day before, at lunch, I'd heard him use the word *sebaceous* in conversation. I had no idea what it meant. I pretended to. I looked it up when no one was looking.

Slowly, tired of being misunderstood, I adapted. I'm not sure I achieved RP, but I certainly mastered FFE (Foreigner Friendly English). In short, moving to Germany was great for my English.

Not everyone was enthusiastic about my new accent and speech patterns, though. I remember phoning home during that first year in Leipzig and having the following conversation with my mother, a woman who proudly describes herself as being as "common as muck". I was telling her a story about a new friend I'd made. She interrupted. "Why u speaking like dat?"

"Like what?"

"Like dat funny *Geeeerman* Inglish."

"What do you mean?" I said. "I'm just speaking normally."

"Naaah, yur not speakin' like, like, propa Inglish. Like wot I speak."

I sighed. "Mum, *propa* doesn't end with an *a*."

29

THE FINE ART OF FINE

I'm new to Germany. It's the first time I'm cooking for my then girlfriend, Annett. I'm a little nervous. I've prepared a carb-heavy monstrosity involving three different forms of potato, and nothing else. British food, then. She's sitting at my kitchen table reading a magazine. She asks if she can help—once.

Just once. I consider this impossibly rude.

The food is ready. I get the tray from the oven. It's so laden with carbohydrate that it weighs as much as an adult dolphin. I put it down in front of her.

We eat. I look at her expectantly.

Nothing happens.

We keep eating. I decide to drop a bigger hint. I nod towards the food.

Nothing happens.

We eat some more. I make some enthusiastic *mmmh* sounds about how delicious the food is.

Nothing happens.

We keep eating. "Do you like it?" I finally ask, abandoning subtlety.

Rather than saying yes automatically, she takes a sip of water. She swallows. "It's fine," she says demurely. Further proof she is the most discourteous person who has ever lived.

"You don't have to eat it if you don't like it. It's no problem. I won't be offended." A lie as large as Kilimanjaro.

"No, it's fine."

"Really? A British person would have complimented it at least ten times by now."

"Oh."

"And are you sure you mean *fine*? *Fine* means, on balance, that you're happier it exists than you would be if it didn't. But are not any more enthusiastic about it than that."

"It does? Oh. I thought it meant it was fine."

"No, it means almost everything else."

"Ah."

"So now you know that, what do you really think about it?"

She pauses. "On balance, I'm happier it exists than I would be if it didn't. But am not any more enthusiastic about it than that."

"I thought you thought it was fine?"

"I was being nice."

"No, you weren't."

"Well I thought I was."

"What are you being now?"

"*German.*"

30

WHAT WE SAY VS WHAT
WE MEAN

I learned quickly in Germany that if there's any chance I might not like the answer, I shouldn't ask the question—there will be no room for interpretation. With us Crumpeters, you're going to have the opposite problem. You're going to ask questions and get answers —and then you'll have to interpret from them what's really meant. As with *fine*, the margins may be, well, fine.

Here's a collection of some of the more common British euphemisms.

What we say	What we really mean	What is understood
"Hello, how are you?"	"Hello."	"Hello, tell me honestly how you are."
"It's *interesting* . . ."	"It's interesting in the same way excrement rolled in glitter would be interesting."	"It's interesting."
"It's not bad."	"It's really very good. Its existence impresses me."	"It's mediocre."
"It's *quite* good."	"It's disappointing."	"It's quite good."
"It's quite *good*."	"It's extremely awesome and I would probably marry it!"	"It's quite good."
"Oh, by the way/Incidentally . . ."	"The primary purpose of our discussion is . . ."	"This is not very important . . ."
"Could we consider some other options?"	"Your idea is the worst since bubble tea. It is dead to me. We're doing something else."	"They have not yet decided."
"I'll bear it in mind."	"I've already forgotten it."	"They will probably do it."
"I'm sure it's my fault."	"It's your fault."	"It's their fault."
"I tend to agree . . ."	"I consider myself to be an agreeable person. However, in this instance, I'm anything but. You are wrong."	"They agree in this instance."
"You're an absolute star."	"You have done my job for me. Thanks, moron."	"They appreciate my contribution."
"In my humble opinion . . ."	"For the sake of diplomacy, I am going to pretend I am humble, and that I say might not be right. It is right."	"They are not absolutely sure about what they are about to say."
"She's quite a character."	"She's awful. I'd cross the road to avoid her."	"She's quite a character."
"He's got a lovely personality."	"He's overweight."	"He's got a lovely personality."
"I hear what you say."	"I'm tired of hearing what you say. Please shut up."	"They accept my point of view."
"Correct me if I'm wrong . . ."	"I'm not wrong. Do not correct me."	"Feel free to tell me your opinion if it differs from mine."
"Do as much as you think is justified."	"Keep doing things until explicitly told you can stop. Then do a bit more anyway."	"Just do what you can/feel like."
"Can I borrow you for a sec?"	"You are in deep, deep shit. Over-your-head deep. This is going to hurt."	"They want a quick chat about something."
"Can I pick your brains about something?"	"Can I steal your ideas and pass them off as my own?"	"They want my help with something."
"When you get a minute."	"Drop everything else. Do it immediately."	"I can do it at a time convenient for me."

31

UNDERSTATEMENT AND
EUPHEMISM

British Airways flight BA 009 is thirty-seven-thousand feet over the Indian Ocean when all four of its engines fail, due to an ash cloud from a nearby volcano. The plane tilts and begins an unexpected descent. Oxygen masks drop down onto terrified passengers' heads. The pilot is a Brit named Eric Moody, who is anything but, and he uses the plane's public-address system to say the following:

"Good evening, ladies and gentlemen. This is your captain speaking. We have a small problem. All four engines have stopped. We are all doing our damnedest to get them going again. I trust you are not in too much distress."

Eric Moody, like so many of my people, is a fan of understatement and euphemism. You may have noticed that the British don't state—we understate. Or, if possible, under-understate. If even that feels too confrontational, we'll err further on the side of caution by prefacing with a whole bunch of sweet-sounding words that, upon reflection, say nothing at all. Other cultures might be happy to call a spade a spade, but we're more inclined to call it a "flat-fronted dirt-redistribution device."

You'll find this kind of understatement in most of our sentences. We don't get fired; we get "let go", "downsized", or "relieved of our duties". You might consider that a disaster, but we're more likely to label it "a spot of bother", or "a trifle disappointing". A situation that leaves us not unemployed but merely "between jobs", a little "out of pocket" or "fiscally challenged". A situation that forces us to admit our circumstances "leave a lot to be desired".

When you're around us, don't just say how it is, accurately, with the truth's sharp edges facing out. Cloister. Wrap reality in poetry, ambiguity, subterfuge, misdirection, and a duvet of euphemism. Be a magician sawing meaning in half, pulling soft, cuddly rabbits of rhetoric out of each sentence's hat. Be Eric Moody having his "small problem" of total engine failure at thirty-seven-thousand feet.

A powerful weapon in the British dark art of euphemism and conversational subterfuge is called *litotes*. It's when, to avoid being too linguistically assertive when appraising something—a person's hat, a new type of strawberry yoghurt, communism—you adopt the opposite position but soften it with a *not*.

Good becomes *not bad*

Bad becomes *not terrible*

I like it becomes *it does not displease me*

Using litotes is *not exactly brain surgery* (it's trivial), even for *not the sharpest* tools in the shed (stupid people), and while it's perhaps *not our favourite linguistic tool* (it's average), and *not without its problems* (it's problematic), all in all, its use is *not too shabby indeed* (it's great).

In conclusion, while I wouldn't say we British leave a lot to be desired, there's no doubt we leave a lot to be interpreted.

OVERSTATEMENT

While we strongly favour understatement, there are specific situations in which we take off our personality strait jackets and go positively praise crazy. Situations where overstatement is encouraged. These are exciting opportunities to release any pent-up life enthusiasm. Don't waste them.

The situations are specific, however. They come about when discussing the following:

1. The previous night's alcohol consumption
Don't say: "I was drunk."
Say: "I was absolutely smashed, completely shitfaced, off my tits. I had no idea what was going on. It was totally epic. I think. I don't remember. Did I mention that? I woke up in a bin. Not my bin, either."

2. Weather of more than fifteen degrees Celsius
Don't say: "What's that orange ball in the sky?"
Say: "Crikey, what a scorcher! I'm taking my top off."

3. People who displease you

Don't say: "She's just not my type." Or, "I don't like him."
Say: "She fell out of the ugly tree and hit every branch on
the way down." Or, "Someone not quite as educated as I
am might go as far as to call him a f****** c***."

4. How hungry/thirsty you are

Don't say: "I'm a little peckish." Or, "I guess liquid refresh-
ment could be nice."
Say: "I'm gagging for a drink." Or, "I'm absolutely dying
of thirst." Or, "I'm hungry enough to eat a horse and then
run after the jockey."

5. How cute something is

Don't say: "The dog is smaller than normal in a way that
pleases."
Say: "OMG that dog is *soooo* adorable I want to eat him
with a spoon. Here, boy. Here, boy. AHHHHHH bless
him. I'm in love."

6. Job titles

Don't say: "I deliver the post."
Say: "I'm Vice-President of Regional Correspondence
Distribution Coordinator Executive Supervisor."

7. When swearing

Don't say: "This carbonara is a bit shit."
Say: "It's absolute wank." Or, "It's utter shite with shite on
top and a side of shitsticks." Or, "Never before have I had
a carbonara this piss-bloody poor."

33

THE TWENTY MOST ANNOYING PHRASES IN THE ENGLISH LANGUAGE

1. "They've moved house." (They've moved their house? How? With a crane?)
2. "Are you taking the piss?" (What would I do with it? It's a real buyers' market for piss right now.)
3. "These *x* are below par." (That's a shame. Maybe they'll get a hole-in-one next time?)
4. "Cup of tea?" (As opposed to a bucket, sombrero, or bathtub of tea?)
5. "I'll get my own back." (Whose back have you been using until now, then? Was it a rental? From Bertz?)
6. "I must be off." (That's unfortunate. Should I turn you on again?)
7. "I'll get the drinks in." (Have they been waiting outside all this time?)
8. "I was gutted." (That seems like an overreaction. Did they think you were a fish?)
9. "Ya know wot I'm sayin'?" (Not really. I think I got distracted by how bad you are at saying it.)

10. "I can't believe it—it was sunny this morning!" (Yeah, because all the previous weather we've had has been so reliable, right?)

11. "I've had it with him." (You've had *it*? Seriously? *It*? Well, I never . . .)

12. "Well, I never . . ." (You never what? Finish your sentences . . . ?)

13. "I told him wot for!" (Why? Were you attempting to confuse him?)

14. "He is well fit!" (As opposed to the more commonly found *unwell* fit?)

15. "That's bang out of order!" (Have you tried banging it back into order again?)

16. "Yes, *your Royal Highness*!"(Better than being a Royal Lowness, I suppose?)

17. "Bob's your uncle." (I've told you a thousand times, I don't have an uncle called Bob!)

18. "I'm not being funny." (Well why the hell not? This is Britain. If we wanted a serious conversation, we'd go to France.)

19. "Don't make a meal out of it." (Can I make a light snack out of it instead, then?)

20. "They've lost the plot." (Was it a printout? Have they retraced their steps? Wait, how can they be sure losing the plot wasn't part of the plot?)

34

DOUBLE SWEAR WORDS

My adopted nation, Germany, is a nation of specialists. It's a place where even qualifications have qualifications. Where you can study for seven years to become a window cleaner. That's lovely. Admirable. But not for us Brits, thanks. We're a haven for generalists, blaggers, middle managers, salespeople, and bankers. We specialise in *services*. Pushing paper. Giving each other fancy titles.

That's not to say we're without specialism. We've just chosen mostly useless, non-academic things to specialise in —trivia, sausage rolls, sarcasm, patriotism, and profanity. Especially profanity. If there were an Olympics for profanity, you'd not get Team GB off the podium. We'd leave with more gold than a rapper's mouth. Our national anthem would blare out so often we'd wear out its MP3.

We just love to swear. And we're good at it. The air in our pubs is one colour—blue. Some of us even throw the most offensive word in the entire English language around as if it were a plush teddy holding a heart that says, "I love you, c***." People we don't know we call mate. Our actual mates? The rules of banter require we refer to them only as mingers, dickheads, or cockwombles.

We have one great advantage in this—the double profanity. We're free to stack insults atop each other like filthy Lego bricks of character assassination and form giant Superinsults. They work equally well for people and situations. It doesn't matter if the words don't fit together. If they don't conjure any obvious mental image. That's almost better, even. We're rewarding creativity here, not poetry or accuracy.

So, pick two insults, shove them together into a compound profanity, aim at your friends, and let fly.

Good luck out there, *Arseballs*.

35

THE TEN COMMANDMENTS OF
BRITISH HUMOUR

Still confused by the subtle, sardonic nature of our funny? Just follow these ten simple rules.

1. Jokes are like rounds—if the last one was at someone else's expense, the next one should be at your own.
2. British humour is like a knife: the sharper the better.
3. Dark comedy > light comedy (dark comedy is like food—not everyone has it).
4. The best joke is the one that the victim doesn't notice was entirely at her expense until fifteen minutes later, on her way home.
5. The less appropriate the moment, the greater the need for comedy. Yes, that includes funerals (so fun that people are dying to get one).
6. The more someone takes himself seriously, the more imperative it is to "cut him down to size." Especially if that person is carrying a clipboard. We cannot abide clipboards.

7. If you think a joke was too mean, or cut too close to the bone, simply add, "Ah, bless them" to its end. All karma is restored.

8. Never, ever show you are offended. Doing so results in a 100x increase in teasing on that issue and probably a new, unflattering nickname to boot.

9. If the mockee shows that she's offended and the mocker (not a hot beverage) says, "Alright mate, it was only a joke," all must be forgiven. To not forgive (or at least pretend to have forgiven) is to reveal yourself as humourless and thus commit social hara-kiri.

10. British humour is like a thief with a bureaucracy fetish: it takes many different forms.

Imagine you enter a room to find a stressed friend doing a very bad job assembling IKEA furniture. To make fun of him, which is your civic duty, you could choose from the following:

A) Self-deprecation (making yourself the butt of the joke): "And I always thought *I* had two left thumbs."

B) Sarcasm (using irony to convey contempt): "I can't work out if you need help with it or it needs help with you."

C) Misdirection (swerve your sentence unexpectedly into a wall): "Do you need help *disassembling* it?"

D) Exaggeration (like, *easily* the most amazing form!): "How does it feel to always be the most incompetent person in a room?"

E) Puns (rely on homonyms—words with multiple meanings): "I haven't seen screwing this inept since I was a teenager."

36

COMEDY = TRAGEDY

A woman gets on a bus holding her baby. The bus driver says, "That's the ugliest baby I've ever seen." Shocked, the woman slams her fare down and takes an aisle seat near the back of the bus. The man sitting next to her senses her agitation and asks what's wrong.

"The bus driver insulted me," she says, fuming.

"Really?" says the man sympathetically. "Why, he's a public servant—he's no right to insult passengers."

"Exactly!" she says.

"You should do something."

"You're right. I will," she says, after contemplation. "I'm going to go back up there and give him a piece of my mind!"

"Great idea," the man says. "Here, let me hold your monkey."

This is both my favourite joke in the world and the perfect encapsulation of British humour. It has everything we like in our comedy, which is just one thing: tragedy. Life wronged this woman when it gave her an ugly baby. Then it let the bus driver needlessly offend her. This left her with a choice: she could accept her situation, or she could kick out against it and confront the bus driver. She decides to fight and in doing so, in that valiant act of defiance, life sucker-punches her once more.

Perfect.

Because we Brits don't like winners. Neither in life nor in humour. Winners aren't one of the pack. Winners make us nervous. Because what if we're not winners? Not everyone can be a winner, right? That would undermine the central premise of winningdom. A better route to self-satisfaction is learning to be a happy loser. That's why all our comedy heroes—Mr Bean, Arthur Steptoe, Basil Fawlty, Del Boy, David Brent—are inept, idiotic failures.

People who make us feel good about ourselves.

A modern example is *An Idiot Abroad*'s Karl Pilkington. Karl is a man who goes places he doesn't want to, has a generally quite shitty time there, and goes home having learned absolutely nothing. This franchise (radio, books, and a TV series) is tragic, and only furthers the negative stereotypes about the British being ignorant, monolingual, culturally insensitive, and scared of self-improvement.

It's a massive hit.

This eulogising of losers is part of what makes our humour unusual. Since we laud losers, we're much more likely to self-deprecate, just to be able to join their club. Our society rewards us for making ourselves the butt of our own jokes. British humour is not about trying to escape our unfavourable circumstances—it's about learning to live within them. Therefore, nothing is sacred; if it's happening, no matter how tragic, it's fair game for mockery.

There's something called nominative determinism.

Research shows that your name, something over which you had no control, influences your career choice. If you've ever met a dentist called Mr Molar, or a doctor called Dolittle, you've experienced this. Although it's not well researched, I believe there must be a cultural equivalent of this—cultural determinism. This same effect, believing your culture has bestowed certain innate talents upon you, makes you develop/refine/specialise in these skills. It sees Chinese people specialising in maths, Ukrainians in programming, Germans in car engines, and Brits in comedy.

We have grown up believing we're the funniest people on earth. That humour is our gift to humanity. It doesn't actually matter if it is our gift, of course—just that we believe that.

We believe that. Completely. Totally. Overwhelmingly.

Because of this belief we joke a lot. It's our cultural crutch helping us hobble through the day and accept what we cannot change, as we play a game we can't win.

THE SERIOUS SIDE OF FUNNY

While there might be some dents in the shiny, bejewelled crown of our culture, while our empire might have seen better days, while our Magna Carta might not be the radical, progressive document it once was, I hope in this chapter I've convinced you that there's still one area where our star shines as bright as it ever has—in our humour.

However, I think it would wrong of me to just leave it there. I could, sure. We're funny. Good for us. But now that I've lived abroad for nearly a decade, and have seen how many other countries handle humour, my opinion about ours has changed, somewhat. We're good at it, that's true. But why we're doing it, why it's such an important part of our culture, well, I'm not sure the reason is benign.

I think we should look at the dark side of British humour.

People think that humour comes from a place of strength. Yet history shows the funniest people are often the saddest, the most depressed, the most insecure. Which makes sense when you consider that humour is such a needy form of expression—one of the few that requires such obvious, constant feedback: laughter. Every joke, pun, or clever play on words is really a subtle question asking its audience, "We're still having fun, right? We're still good?"

A society where everyone makes jokes all the time is not necessarily something to be envied. Especially if you use the jokes to be mean, or to cajole and control others. Several academics and researchers have suggested that this is the real reason for humour. That behind those jokes, behind that innocent teasing, the pub banter, we're communicating serious messages. In his book *Laughter and Ridicule: Towards a Social Critique of Humour*, Professor Michael Billig suggests that humour is really about ridicule, and ridicule is about a group upholding their cultural norms.

This is British humour to a T.

An example. Say John notices his friend Bill always shirks his round duties, is ever reluctant to put his hand in his wallet. John has a conundrum. He could confront Bill directly. But that would be risky, might be perceived as rude, confrontational. Bill might get offended. Yet, John doesn't want to keep paying for skinflint Bill.

The solution? *Humour.*

John can use jokes to subtly (or not so subtly) tell Bill to correct his behaviour. John makes sure there are some friends around to hear, and then he teases Bill about how "his wallet must have cobwebs". The group laughs and joins in. One friend quips, "It's ironic he's called Bill." They give him the nickname "Doesn't Get The".

Now, of course, the group does this in a loving, banterous way. With their eyes, their tone, their warm smiles, they're saying, *We like you, Bill. You're one of us.*

Yet behind those funny, innocent-sounding words, there's a coded threat: *Sure, Bill, but for how long?*

CHAPTER 5

"The British Food Pyramid"

Our Cuisine

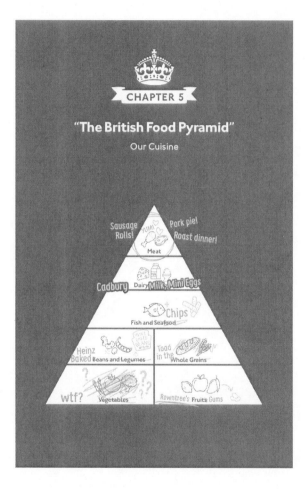

MORE IS MORE

"Less is more," the British expression says.

There are some areas in life where this true —tax bills, mothers-in-law, back hair, etc. But, equally, there are some areas where more is more—privileges, hedonism, baked beans.

And, of course, food.

For us Royalty Enthusiasts, a balanced diet means not eating so much we fall over. We're *quantity* people trapped in a *quality* world. A world that wants things dignified, refined, specialised, exotic. How boring. Anyone can like things that are good. That's easy. We want more of a challenge. We prefer liking things that won't like us back; dirty, exploitative things that want to hurt us, challenge us, clog us, rot us from our insides out. We want everything that's edible in a twenty-metre radius heaped into a mound, fried, and served to us in a bucket.

Other countries have cuisines. We have carbohydrates. If our body doesn't sigh, shudder, or attempt to flee upon sight of it, we know it's not worth putting in our mouths. We've an underdeveloped sense of taste and an overdeveloped sense of gluttony. It's no surprise that Britain is the fattest place in Europe. *No shit*, we thought when we heard that. Who cares. *Have a chip.*

WELCOME TO BRITISH COOKING SCHOOL

LESSON 1
Turn on the deep fat fryer.

LESSON 2
Congratulations, you're done.
Here is your certificate.
Good luck out there, Chef!

SUPER
DEEP FRYER 6100

We don't favour diversity, variety, ecological sustainability—we're in it for heft. We want forty-seven parts of six animals squashed together in a blender, fried, covered in gravy, and served in a bread roll. We want our lunch to be as tall as a toddler. To have the nutritional value of cardboard but the fun-score value of a day out at a culinary theme park.

As a result, eating with us is a delight. All our food tastes fantastic because it's stuffed full of the legal limit of everything flavour enhancing—oil, salt, sugar, MSG. Our supermarkets are wondrous Willy Wonka lands of lost logic and super-convenience where you can buy sliced apple wrapped in plastic, or fresh mash, or a ready-meal roast dinner. All pre-prepared, pre-packed, and pre-posterous. *Just add mouth.*

So, when you're with us, let go. Relax. Forget about the future. Forget about the Food Pyramid. Forget everything you've ever learned about nutrition. Forget you're full already. When it comes to consumption, you're one of us now, and we know: more is more.

39

HAM, EGG, AND CHIPS

There's no clearer example of the undistinguished British palate than ham, egg, and chips—a stalwart of pub menus, a national favourite, a perennial crowd-pleaser of just three ingredients! Not even complementary ingredients. A dish so uncool, rappers don't diss it. A dish so boring, paint watches it dry. A dish so lacking in nutrition, Oliver Twist wouldn't ask for more of it.

I've often wondered how chefs react to it being ordered. This is how I imagine it.

A waiter enters the kitchen and pins the order up on the board. Needing to take a garlic-bread starter to table 12, he turns to leave.

"What's this?" the chef shouts after him.

The waiter turns to find the chef holding the piece of paper aloft. He cocks his head. "One ham, egg, and chips."

The chef scrunches the paper into a ball. "Who put that on the menu, Greg? We've talked about this."

Greg shrugs. "I don't know."

"Do you think I wear this uniform for fun, Greg?"

"No."

"I trained for this, Greg. I'm a chef. A culinary conjuror, a nourishment necromancer, an appetite artiste. I've dedicated my life to the edible. My profession to the palatable. I know the Latin name for "sweet potato", Greg —*Ipomoea batatas*. I know eighteen distinct ways to serve ginger. Asking me to prepare a meal of ham, egg, and chips is like asking Beethoven to compose a jingle for bleach, Greg. *Ham, egg, and chips*. It's not a dish, Greg. It just doesn't work. It's unrelated fried things bunched together on a sad plate of regret."

Greg backs nervously towards the exit. "Yeah, but the beans help—"

"Don't get me started on baked beans, Greg. Don't open that door."

Greg sighs. "We're just giving the people what they want."

A frying pan soars across the room, hits the cowering waiter, and clatters to the ground. An egg slides off it and onto the floor, where it cuddles up to some ham, and a chip.

THE SUNDAY ROAST

I n a recent poll about things the British love about Britain, one special, sacred Sunday ritual took second place. No, it wasn't church. Although we take this ritual so seriously it's almost a religion.

It was the Holy British Sunday Roast.

Heaven on earth. What better description of bliss could there be than "a heaped plate of gravy-soaked, roasted wonder"? Way more enticing than any pearly gates or harp-playing angel. You can't eat a pearly gate, after all. Or fry a harp. You might be able to roast an angel, but it's probably frowned upon.

Preparing a British roast is simple: take a plate, then bury it in vegetables, meat, and roast potatoes. What vegetables? It doesn't matter. They're just the window dressing, there to make you feel less guilty about all the meat and potatoes you're about to consume. How many potatoes? Enough to sink the ark. Now submerge that ark in gravy.

Go on, really drown it . . .

Okay, you're nearly there.

Next, top the meal with its crowning achievement: the Yorkshire pudding. Godly, sanctified little saucers of roasted dough, peas be upon them. A roast without Yorkshire puddings is like a bank without money—a waste of everyone's time. Getting the Yorkshire right will take a few decades of practice, so you'd best get started. Consistency is everything. You want it not too crispy, not too soft. Devouring it should be like chewing on a bouncy castle of candy floss squelching in a delicious puddle of warm gravy.

Done? Ready to serve? Show me your plate . . .

What's that, in the corner? Is that ceramic I see? *Fail.* Hang your head in shame. Get on the Eurostar. You're done. I don't even want to look at you.

And are you carrying it with one hand?! *Double fail.* Add more food, now, before someone sees.

The plate should look like the messy end of a game of Food Jenga in which the aim was succumbing to gastric distress. Looking at the plate, overflowing in food, should make your eyes exclaim "Fuck yes!" and your stomach say "Seriously, boss? I mean, I'll give it a good go, but I'm not promising anything".

41

GREGGS

I f you go down to a British high street today, you're in for a treat. Nestled next to the familiar names—Pret, McDonald's, and Starbucks—you'll find a new, uniquely British success story. A chain that has come out of nowhere (Newcastle, to be more specific) to sweep its adversaries into the bin.

This famously low-priced chain is called Greggs. An establishment where the Food Pyramid is not merely inverted but smashed to pieces before your eyes, deep-fried, and force-fed to you.

Ostensibly, Greggs is just a bakery. A place of bread. Of things wrapped in pastry and baked. Nothing spectacular. Nothing new. Nothing nutritious. Yet, somehow, Greggs *is* more. Its food tastes better, costs less, and fills you up longer than is rationally understandable. A sort of carb voodoo takes place there. A taste hex.

This new chain is extraordinarily successful. So much so that 1698 of them now clog up the arteries of my nation's shopping streets—more than any other fast food chain. Greggs sells two and a half million a week. In the time it took you to read that sentence it sold another four. One newspaper food critic described Greggs as "good stuff, with the caveat that you are talking about massive amounts of carbohydrate". He didn't seem to notice he'd just described the entirety of British cuisine. A cuisine Greggs now rules. You can even find them inside of hospitals, the equivalent of putting an active volcano inside a kindergarten. Upon hearing that the Greggs branch inside New Cross Hospital in Wolverhampton (where 70 percent of the population is obese) is the second busiest in the country, in an act of wonderful British understatement, the *Guardian* reported the local NHS boss as saying the situation was "not ideal".

As a student, I regularly visited Greggs because you could buy a steak bake for forty-seven pence and be full for three days afterward. I only go there now to people-watch. It's like a foray into foolishness. I observe people gorging on the Spicy Chicken and Pepperoni Lattice (just 463 calories!) accompanied by a side sausage roll (a mere 326 more), garnished with a Grab Bag pack of salt and vinegar crisps, and washed down with a Diet Coke. *Yes, a Diet Coke.* Because you've got to take care of yourself, haven't you? Adding a Diet Coke to a meal like that is like dropping a pack of plasters down with a nuclear bomb. You're just adding insult to injury.

If you think I'm exaggerating, I've a challenge—enter the next Greggs you see (they won't be hard to find; on a day's sightseeing you'll see so many you'll think they're stalking you). Inside, you must spend £2.70 on food (the average transaction price in a Greggs). Sounds easy, but it won't be. Their prices are as low as their calories are high.

Now, you must eat all that food in one sitting. If you can do that, congrats, you're British. If you feel guilty after, it's okay—there's always Diet Coke.

42

CHIP SHOPS

At the height of our empire, we owned most of the world and were surrounded by the planet's most interesting spices. They were ours. We could just take them. We didn't even have to pay.

Did we take them? Did we get a bit curious? Did we dabble?

No.

Why would we? We already had salt and pepper—the dynamic duo, the taste tornado, the flavour fellowship. The topic was closed. Perfection had been reached.

Today, things have improved slightly. While we've branched out a little, our taste tree remains spartan. Ask us to name spices and watch us struggle to reach five. Ask us to name fizzy drinks, however, and watch us effortlessly reel off thirty.

Salt and pepper remain the undisputed king and queen of our plates. And what do we like drenching in them most?

Fish and chips.

In researching the Great British Fish and Chip Shop

(I've a challenging job, I know), I came across something called the National Federation of Fish Friers. Yep, you read that correctly. There is a National Federation of Fish Friers. People whose speciality is dropping fish into hot oil, letting it sit there a little while, then lifting it out again, wrapping it in old news, and handing it to someone who should know better.

They must have some fascinating general meetings. I hope they keep detailed minutes.

Thanks to their nutritious online presence, I now know that there are 8500 fish and chip shops in the UK, eight for every McDonald's. I know that 10 percent of the nation's potato crop is used (some might say squandered) by them. That the fish and chip industry is worth 1.2 billion pounds a year to our economy. That 22 percent of the nation visits a fish and chip shop at least once a week. That they are our most popular takeaway.

Now you know those things, too. They are irrefutable evidence that this is one of those stereotypes that's true. *We love fish and chips.*

I knew that already from growing up in my small British town. We lived so near to such a shop—an accident, my parents insist—that we could see it from the upstairs windows. If my mum didn't have time to cook (I'm using *cook* in its most liberal form here to mean *to fry or sandwich something*), we kids would be sent out to Fry's Chip Shop, with eighty pence in our hand, to get a chip butty. This was considered acceptable parenting. Social services didn't arrive unannounced to inspect our teeth for signs of malnourishment. It was a more innocent time, I guess.

Oh, I'd probably better explain what a chip butty is. I hope you're sitting down. Are you sitting down?

Sit down . . .

A chip butty is a baffling carbception. It's taking a bad

idea (eating a meal that consists of just fried potato) then wrapping it in a bread roll. Carbs being the only thing the meal didn't need more of, of course. And just in case you think we've reached peak insanity—*the roll is buttered*. You heard that right. Buttered! Like taking buckets of water to a flood. In certain parts of the North and Scotland, there's a weirder local adaptation called a pie barm. Which is a pie served in a bread roll. And you thought the National Federation of Fish Friers was absurd.

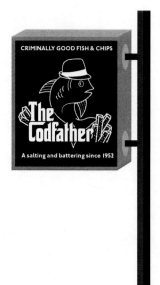

CRIMINALLY GOOD FISH & CHIPS

The Codfather

A salting and battering since 1952

43

SANDWICHING

While in Mexico, I had the chance to watch turtles hatching on a beach; a beautiful sight. After they hatch, baby turtles automatically make a swimming motion with their tiny little limbs. On land, this motion works as a crawl and is what gets them from the beach into the ocean. If you pick them up, they continue thrashing the air.

All species have adaptive behaviours like this—instincts, survival traits, automatic reflexes. Throw a dog in water and it starts to swim. It didn't know it knew how to swim. And yet it finds itself able to swim.

We humans have these traits too. We blink, we pull away when we touch something hot, we laugh at people when they fall over. What is less known, however, is that we Brits have been bestowed with an additional, special adaptive behaviour: *sandwiching*.

British people left alone for more than a minute automatically begin making sandwiches. Just like the dog and the turtle, they won't even know they're doing it. They won't be able to explain it. They can't help it. It's an instinct. Or a compulsion, perhaps.

Long ago, we realised that everything in life is better when it's wrapped in the soft embrace of bread. Since then, we've been busy sandwiching everything we could get our mitts on (even pies).

It doesn't matter if we're not hungry, or if there's nothing edible around. We'll improvise. Leave us in a meeting room while you nip to the toilet, and upon return, you'll find we've wrapped the stapler between two manila folders, buttered with coffee. It's better now, isn't it? Yes, it is.

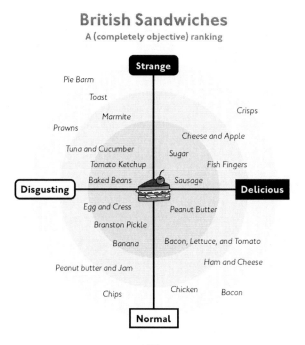

British Sandwiches
A (completely objective) ranking

Strange

Pie Barm

Toast

Crisps

Marmite

Prawns

Cheese and Apple

Tuna and Cucumber   Sugar

Tomato Ketchup   Fish Fingers

Baked Beans   Sausage

Disgusting   **Delicious**

Egg and Cress   Peanut Butter

Branston Pickle

Banana   Bacon, Lettuce, and Tomato

Ham and Cheese

Peanut butter and Jam

Chips   Chicken   Bacon

Normal

123

44

CRISP SANDWICHES

Spend enough time amongst us and someone is going to offer to make you the most special of all sandwiches—*a crisp sandwich*.

Yes, a sandwich with crisps in it. You heard right.

You're going to say no, because, *a sandwich with crisps in it?!*

They're going to insist. You're going to resist. They're going to insist some more. You're going to give in. After all, you're in their home; it's their country; their culture; their rules.

They will reach for the oldest bread they have.

You will take your head in your hands. You can't watch. How old is that bread? Days, weeks, months, perhaps even years old?

Don't worry, foreigner. Our bread is so soft, light, and artificial that it doesn't mould or stale. It's immortal. It's vampire yeast.

Next, they're going to butter this thousand-year-old Dracula bread. Oh, how they're going to butter it! The butter will be so thick you could skid on it. Write your name in it. Lie down and thrash around in it.

You peek between your fingers. Are they really doing this?

They are.

They open a packet of crisps. Ready salted, perhaps. Roast chicken, maybe. Salt and vinegar, ideally; the Elvis of crisps. They might add something else to the sandwich mix—a slice of ham? But probably not. It's already perfect, after all.

They place that sandwich in front of you.

You remove your hands from your face. You look down at this abomination. You frown. Scepticism overwhelms you, becomes you.

They nod down at it.

You sigh. Timidly, you pick it up and place a corner into your mouth. You begin to chew. It will be an ordeal, you think, because that bread is older than the Bible. But then it just dissolves, hugging your taste buds. It's the tremendous amount of butter, no doubt. Your teeth meet a crisp that yields with just the lightest, most joyous little snap.

The rough.

The smooth.

The combination.

It's like eating joy that's been sequestered in silk and slathered with love.

Your mouth shudders. It's a jaw orgasm. You "mmmmm" loudly, a little too loudly; you're self-conscious about it. It's just a crisp sandwich. Not exactly Michelin-star worthy. So then why does it make you feel like this? So infatuated. So . . . in love at first bite. You devour another mouthful. You apologise to your host, as you should.

Crisp sandwiches are a triumph.

CHEDDAR

W hy do the French have so many types of cheese? Because they can't get cheddar right.

MARMITE

I'm sure you know the legend of the Sword in the Stone, in which King Arthur frees Excalibur, proving himself rightful king of England.

What you might not know, however, is that a similar test of cultural pedigree occurs in every British kitchen, every morning. A challenge involving a modern-day Excalibur, in the form of a curious black sludge beloved by exactly 50 percent of my nation-folk: *Marmite*.

The challenge is as follows: having innocently dipped our knives into this gunk, with our warm toast waiting, we Brits must prise our knives back out of this sticky breakfast bog, where it sits as firmly as Arthur's sword once sat in the stone.

Marmite likes our knives.

Marmite thinks it might keep them.

A tug of war ensues. Toast gets tepid. Only those of a pure British cultural sensitivity succeed in freeing their cutlery to move on, victorious, to the first challenge of their new reign: spreading this sticky, lumpy tar across their soft, white, rubbish British bread. Bread wholly unprepared for what is about to follow, like a clown who's accidentally unicycled, while juggling, into a blizzard.

Marmite became popular when, during the Second World War, the nation found its cupboards bare. In the corner—dusty and marked *??!!??*—were a few vats of Marmite. Out of other options, Brits started putting it in soldiers' ration boxes. Marmite took its chance spectacularly, smudging itself thickly over the gums of the soldiers. Compared to what they'd endured, what they'd seen, what they'd had to eat (or not eat), they probably found Marmite only *mostly awful*, at first. That was enough. It worked for them. Over time, they became indifferent to it. Then apathetic. Then, suddenly, almost against their will, they found themselves starting to look forward to it. To want it. Then, lastly, they realised *they liked it*. They couldn't explain why. On paper, nothing about it appealed. But on bread? Well, nothing either, and yet still they craved it. Needed it.

They returned home, addicted, to indoctrinate their families.

Families like mine. After moving to Germany and finding my supply cut, I began importing it from eBay. I think it tastes simultaneously of home, childhood and, salt. Salt, mostly—since, like everything we Brits love, it seems Marmite also wants to kill us. I haven't checked, but I think its ingredients are petrol, glue, melted-down shopping trolleys, and horse face.

Along with its distinctive taste, it's most known for its tag line: "You either love it or hate it." Which conveniently forgets that there are other options, such as, "It will kill you before you've formed a firm opinion."

TEA

I f you've ever watched football, you'll know that when a player gets injured, a physio runs on from the side and attends the injury with a wet sponge.

It's called, semi-ironically, the magic sponge.

How it works is not magic. It works because, well, it's a placebo. The injured player feels he's getting medical attention; the physio feels she's doing something. The player gets up ~~better~~ wetter and the game continues.

Life has a lot of magic sponges, it turns out. Things that work because we believe in them: lucky numbers, horoscopes, homeopathy, soulmates.

We Island Monkeys have our own special version of this sponge: the magic kettle. Just like that physio, we love nothing more than rushing out from the sidelines of everyday British life to fix any injury, slight, scorn, fatigue, or embarrassment by pouring warm, caffeinated, calming tea upon it. We understand that tea is an all-purpose salve for the human condition. In fact, just saying the sentence "How about I make us a nice cup of tea?" is known to instantly relieve 50 percent of world weariness and existence-fatigue symptoms. Not that we need a specific reason to drink tea. Lack of tea was the problem tea was created to solve, after all.

No matter the day, no matter the tragedy, no matter the time, no matter the thoughts or feelings, there is simply no situation that cannot be improved with a nice cuppa. Tea is not about the liquid. Tea is about the ritual of tea. About the ceremony of tea. About taking time out. About caring for each other. It's a marker of existence, of time passing. It's the way we bond. Other cultures break bread—we brew tea. Then we get up better, warmer, calmer, caffeinated, thoroughly biscuited (ideally), and the game of life continues.

IRN-BRU

Perhaps the strangest drink amongst my kin is the bright-orange carbonated monstrosity Irn-Bru. While it's a beverage you can find in all corners of our land, it's the Scots who birthed this mutant, sickly redhead and remain its proud, passionate parents. They delight in telling you that there are only two countries in the world where the top-selling drink isn't Coca-Cola; Scotland is one of them, and Irn-Bru is that drink. It's liquid defiance, fizzy independence, orange originality. It's most famed for its colour, which is 94 percent more ginger than anything occurring in nature.

If you've ever tasted it (no doubt a dark chapter in your life), you've probably concluded that the ever-patriotic Scots are buying it out of national pride, not enjoyment of its absurd taste. On the streets of Edinburgh and Glasgow, people are politely pretending to take sips from it but then secretly pouring it into the nearest plant when no one is looking. A plant that dies instantly, having been poisoned by this weird tangerine, saccharine mucus.

If nationalistic pride is not the reason for its popularity, it could be that Scots swear it has magical, wondrous hang-over-destroying abilities. In the interest of science—and after an evening of one too many gin tonics—I tested this quack cure. In my tender morning-after state, I did find that Irn-Bru had a strange effect on my fragile physiology. It didn't make me feel better, exactly, but *different*. I don't think Irn-Bru relieves the dull aches of excess but does succeed in confusing the body with a sharp attack of syrupy distraction. It simply *WTF*s it. The body goes from being mad at you to being too confused to form any strong conclusions right now. It'll check in again later, whenever this bizarre, tangy taste-bud Fukushima has passed.

THE DRINKING OLYMPICS

Who would want to be an athlete? All the monotonous training, special diets, early mornings, and bad pay? And for what? A career that's over by your mid-thirties? And all that doping?

You'd have to be a dope to do it, really, wouldn't you?

Luckily, we Brits understand that there are many forms of athleticism. Accordingly, we've taken the basic spirit of the Olympics—spectacle, one-upmanship, skin-tight clothing—and improved upon it by creating a special late-night version: the Drinking Olympics.

A Drinking Olympics can be called by anyone, at any time, and always begins with the same six words—"Shall we go for a drink?"

If a British person ever says this phrase to you, *run*. Run for your sanity. Run for your wallet. Run for your life and liver.

It's the most disingenuous statement in the entirety of the English language. Right up there with "It was lovely to meet you", "Let's agree to disagree", and, "It's fine". If you're foolish enough to agree to this suggestion, the Olympic torch is lit, the starter gun is fired, and the games are open. A Drinking Olympics has begun. You're to be one of the competitors.

"Go for a drink?" Singular? Pah! What the person really means, of course, is go for a drink (opening ceremony), sneak through a mass of bodies to the bar (slalom), down some shots (shot put), set a five-round personal bar-best (round relay), add Baileys to drinks that aren't improved in any way by the addition of Baileys (curdles), rush off to the toilet (100-metre sprint), get into a heated argument with someone who "looks at you funny" (twatkondo), and have a drunken fumble with someone near the toilets (hand-to-ball) before going for some chips (synchronised carbing), trying to stay up upright while hailing a taxi (ginnastics), falling over (floor ginnastics), vomiting in the back of the taxi on the way home (stomach judo), a home you momentarily fail to locate then take five minutes opening the door of (lockchery), before waking up, taking some aspirin (doping), having a fry-up (table toast-nis), and calling that a successful Tuesday night's games.

Watching us, you can only conclude we're in a decades-long war with our own livers.

And that we're winning.

The Drinking Olympics

ALCOHOL GREMLINS

While we are enthusiastic participants in the Drinking Olympics, we are not very skilled athletes. Even though we train from a young age, under the tutelage of Carling, Smirnoff, and Gordon's, we're good at alcohol in the same way psychopaths are good team players, children excel at algebra, and the Amish nail e-mail: we might understand the general concept, but that doesn't mean we get the execution right. We're the Eddie the Eagle of binge drinking.

Keeps calm and carries on

Flips out and removes clothes

Do you remember the hit nineties franchise Gremlins? In it were cute, lovable, fluffy, polite little creatures that had just one flaw—they couldn't get wet. If they did, they turned into savages. Well, that's us. That's exactly us. We Brits are alcohol gremlins.

Sober, we're delightful. Friendly, warm, charming, non-confrontational. But get our livers wet—about three pints should do it—and we'll transform before your disbelieving eyes. Our primitive urges and base instincts take over. For a while, we're still civilised. Funnier, even. We're putting our glass on our head. Flirting with the next table. Singing. Ordering rounds of shots for the bar. Then that third pints passes through our fragile physiology, and the switch is hit.

We go full gremlin. We get paranoid. Aggressive. Innocent remarks are misconstrued. We're bumping into people. Is that person "looking at us?" There are confrontations. Yes, con*front*ations. Con*back*tations are for the sober. Innocent flirting becomes a cruder "hitting on" (often in both senses of the word). Our hair gets unkempt, our clothes come off. We bare our teeth and other body parts. It gets ugly.

When I was a student, because of alcohol gremlins, I used to avoid walking through Nottingham city centre on Friday and Saturday nights. It was too rough, the odds of getting caught in random violence too high. Even if I avoided that, the other things I'd see—the vomiting in bins, the throwing of bins, the sex in doorways, the smashing of bus stops, the roving gangs of plastered proletariat—were enough to make me want to hide at home with the duvet over my head and an Enid Blyton book on my lap. If you've seen the zombie-apocalypse movie *28 Days Later*, you'll have some idea of what it was like.

3 pints later, they should have called it.

THE MORNING-AFTER MEDAL
CEREMONY

The excesses of the night before might be over, but the next morning, everything is still up for grabs. It's still possible to cover yourself in glory. Win a medal. Grab a spot atop the podium of debauchery. Because it's time for the morning-after medal ceremony, where Olympians come together to congratulate each other—usually over an oily cooked breakfast—on the previous night's feats.

To take part, you must remember the exact number of beverages you consumed and the nature of each (when in doubt, double the figure and triple the exoticism). Next, describe in detail what hurts (everything), how much it hurts (significantly), how ashamed you are of how badly you behaved (you're faking this—you're proud, very proud), and how little you remember of what occurred (try to have forgotten everything, including your own name).

Touch your forehead a lot.

Make numerous loud murmuring sounds.

Really ham it up.

Certain things will earn you a good score with the

judges: ending up in hospital (God bless the NHS); being paralytic; getting into a fight; having "gotten off" with or "pulled" someone (especially if this person is considered less attractive than you); having spent a lot of money (especially if you have receipts from a place you don't remember going to); returning with someone else's clothing (underwear scores double); and having slept somewhere else (wheelie bin, hedge, stranger's bed).

I remember a night out with my university flatmates at a notoriously awful Australian-themed bar called Outback. Why anything needs to be Australian themed is a mystery to me. I'm not even sure Australia should be, but I'm digressing. It was a typical night out in Nottingham. By its end, one flatmate had been sexually assaulted; another had had her purse stolen. And Johnny got so drunk he fell asleep on the toilet, in the basement of the club, and woke up at 5am to bouncers banging on its door. He came to, had no idea where he was, and looked down to find he'd vomited all over himself, including inside his trousers, which were down round his ankles. He then pulled them up and squelched in them all the way home.

He told us this story with pride, over breakfast, during the morning-after medal ceremony. We threw in our misdemeanours, too. They didn't compare. They were silver or bronze, at best. Johnny was the winner. Had set a record in stupidity. He took the gold. Took the accolades and top spot on the podium.

It was concluded that, all in all, the night had been a great success. So good, in fact, that we'd repeat it again the next night. Although not at Outback. We had standards.

CHAPTER 6

"A game of two halves"

Sports, Hobbies, and the Everyday

British national sports

❶ Football ❷ Rugby ❸ Holding doors open
❹ Being sarcastic ❺ Bantering ❻ Talking about the weather
❼ Talking about talking about the weather
❽ Asking whose round it is, whilst knowing exactly
whose round it is
❾ Saying sorry, please or thank you

52

WETHERSPOONS

I t's Tuesday night. You've had a hard day at work. Time to stop in at your "local", The King's Head. You haven't drunk or been drunk anywhere else in years. Inside, before the door is even closed, Tracey has already started pouring your usual. She's a keeper, that Tracey. At the bar you spot your friends, "the regulars". A crew every bit as lovely as they are motley. You've drunk, laughed, loved, and lamented together for years yet still only know each other by your nicknames: Secret Asian Chris (lactose intolerant), Little John (called John and very tall), Big Little John (also called John, but short), Barry Potter (called Barry and a wizard with cars), and Scary Spiced (Indian).

As you approach the bar, the pub dog, Cat, rushes up to you. You look over to the corner and see that *your* chair, in front of the open fire, is free. The jukebox plays an REM song you've heard seven thousand times. You whistle along. You're at home. No, better, for your home doesn't have Guinness on tap.

It's a great night. It's always a great night at The King's Head.

The next two weeks are busy with work. Finally, you get another spare evening. You've missed King's. Turning the corner, you look up and see the sign has gone. That's weird. You look at the building's facade. Was it always this colour? Cobalt blue? With silver stripes? What's going on? Above the door, there's a tasteful, minimalist black sign with *Matterhorn* written on it in a hand-drawn font.

Oh no they didn't . . .

Inside, it's as dark as any cave. Copper pipes have been installed. You have the suspicion someone nearby is *craft brewing*.

You shudder.

The carpet underfoot isn't sticky anymore, because there isn't carpet anymore. It's all exposed, naked, vulnerable wood. At the bar, where Tracey should be, good old Tracey, Tracey the keeper, there's a two-metre-tall moustachioed Scandinavian hipster called Kurt, in red dungarees. He smiles and pours you a Moscow mule in a beaker, with ice balls.

You heard right. Ice balls.

Your eyes water. It's either the price or his aftershave. Barry Potter is nowhere to be seen.

They did it to your pub, too! Another old-school, no-nonsense, unpretentious British boozer has shut. They're all shutting. These institutions, a core part of our brand and fame, are now in decline, failing to compete with the choice, specialism, and transience offered by cities, failing to find enough regulars in dying rural areas that are still satisfied with warm Carling, REM, and ham, egg, and chips. The King's Head is merely the latest to fall.

You call up Little John. "We're in 'Spoons," he says.

You can't believe what you're hearing. *Spoons? Wetherspoons?!*

Wetherspoons is the nation's biggest and most loved-to-hate pub chain, and the only one still growing, with a thousand venues offering cheap, no-frills boozing. The Ryanair of alcohol.

Having fled Matterhorn, you arrive at 'Spoons, in a corner of the town square. Inside, you find it packed. A swirling mass of Guinness and Strongbow–powered barflies, hipsters, after-workers, young lovers, and old lamenters. A true social melting pot, just the way it should be.

"It's always like this, apparently," Little John says. You spot a few familiar faces. There's no jukebox—Wetherspoons is too tight to splurge on a music licence. But that's not the end of the world as you know. You feel fine. You take a seat. Look around. Everyone's here. Over five pints (for just twelve pounds!), the seeds of three fights, one round of food poisoning, four one-night stands, two love affairs, one marriage, and twelve visits to A&E germinate. Does the barman know your name? No. Is there a dog called Cat? Nope. But at 'Spoons, you can at least afford to drown your sorrows, rather than just dip their toes in Moscow mules.

53

BEER JACKETS

Y ou might have heard the rumour that the weather in Britain is rather underwhelming. I'd like to make a joke now about Britain always having four seasons in one day, but there's just not enough summer to justify it. British summers ripen like an Avocado: they're not ready . . . not ready . . . not ready . . . and . . . *too late*. I'm not sure you can blink and miss them, but you can certainly take a nap in late spring and wake up in early autumn.

If you've seen us on a night out, you'll understand that we've adapted to our climate mediocrity. We don't let our bad weather faze us. You'll have seen our women, mini-skirted and high-heeled, trying not to fall over and break their ankles on icy pavements. Or groups of us lads, our shoulders wrapped around high around our heads, bracing ourselves against biting winds as we queue in our bright shirts to get into a club. You probably thought we were cold, right? Just because we were shivering, one giant goosebump, and our lips looked on loan from Blue Man Group?

Wrong.

We were perfectly warm enough. Snuggly. Toasty. If anything, we were regretting wearing such a large mini-skirt. That's because we're heated by an alternative source of energy that less hardy, overseas types don't have access to; a magic item of invisible clothing for the night-time partying emperor.

It's called a Beer Jacket.

We Brits understand that you're only going to be cold if you're not drunk enough. Each beer is worth two degrees.

In many ways, Beer Jackets are actually superior to the real thing since they go with anything, you never have to pay to put them in the cloakroom, they still fit if you gain eight (a process they are more than happy to assist with), and they don't get dirty when you fall off the kerb into a muddy puddle at 3am. Several countries have the expression "There's no such thing as bad weather, just bad clothing". For us, it's the opposite; there's no bad clothing, just bad weather. And bad weather is a problem we can easily fix. So get another round in—it's getting nippy . . .

BINGO

You probably like games, right? The excitement, the uncertainty, getting to slip into a fantasy world where you're the landlord of Park Lane and can extract significant taxes from your git of a younger brother's illegally parked steamboat?

Sure you do.

But some parts of game playing aren't very good, are they? The complicated rules; the falling out with each other; the cheating; the feeling stupid when you don't know the capital of Botswana or the chemical symbol for magnesium; the effort required for active games like charades, where you're reduced to describing things with your body parts, like a pop-culture cheerleader.

Ugh.

Which is why We of The Sandwich have perfected, popularised, commercialised, and become enamoured with a special game. A better game. A purer game. A game that, also, *isn't*. A Game Zero, without effort additives and trivia preservatives. A game you can play no matter how drunk you are. A game you can play sitting down. A game you can chat during. A game entirely devoid of strategy. A game where you get to use a massive pen called a "dabber". How often in life do you get to use a massive pen? *Exactly.* It's to life's detriment that its pens are so narrow-nibbed.

This special game fixes that.

Fixes all game problems.

Fixes all problems, now that I think about it . . .

It's called bingo.

Ostensibly, bingo is a simple, skill-less game where someone at the front of the room calls out a number, and if you have that number on your bingo card, you mark it with the dabber. Should all your numbers come up, or a special formation of numbers, like the four corners, you win a prize. Money, most likely. The best prize. For it allows you to buy more bingo cards, play more bingo, and thus use more dabbers.

Each night, thousands play along in bingo halls across the country, sitting in little booths, next to a lucky charm plush toy or two. It has been this way for a century.

But in 2014, we learned that three-quarters of our bingo halls had closed over the past thirty years. Somehow, no one had noticed bingo's failing to keep up with the dynamism, intrigue, and thrill of modern-day games. Or any game, really. Or watching grass grow.

But the British need their beloved bingo. Something would have to be done. Our chancellor passed a special law that lowered tax on bingo profits from 20 percent to 10 percent. We would protect our bingo halls as if they were an endangered exotic river dolphin of late-night hedonism. Because bingo is the best of us: egalitarian; inclusive; easily combinable with alcohol. An effortless, transcendental, nirvana-game-state for the strategy- and trivia-hating masses.

British Cliché Bingo

... DOWN THE PUB	TO BE FAIR	IT'S A NIGHTMARE!	SO SORRY.
WHOSE ROUND?	TO BE HONEST	... HAS GONE PEAR-SHAPED	
REALLY?	RIGHT THEN ...	IT'S POLITICAL CORRECTNESS GONE MAD.	
CALM DOWN, WE WERE ONLY HAVING A LAUGH.		CUP OF TEA, ANYONE?	
NAH, MATE.	WHAT ABOUT THIS WEATHER WE'VE BEEN HAVING LATELY?		
... IS THE DOG'S BOLLOCKS	HOW ARE YOU? I'M FINE, THANKS. YOU?		
WHEN ALL'S SAID AND DONE	AT THE END OF THE DAY ...	... ISN'T IT?	
BASICALLY	THE PROPERTY LADDER	AT THIS MOMENT IN TIME ...	

Try to use all these cliché phrases
in just one day. Good luck.

55

CRICKET

When foreigners encounter the curious, unfathomable sport of cricket, their usual reaction is *I don't understand it*. Don't worry, that's normal. While I've never played the game, I do have a British passport, so I'm qualified to explain it. It works like this.

Cricket is played by men, because women have better things to do with their time. It needs two teams of eleven men and a reserve. Each team "bats" while the other team "fields". It's called fielding because you stand in a field. You might think it's called batting because you bat, but mostly you don't bat. You pretend. Which means those who are fielding don't really get to field. But that's not their fault.

Batsmen bat at something called a "crease". It isn't creased. It's straight. A bowler "bowls" the ball, which means he throws it as fast as he can, over arm, trying to hit the batsman's "wicket", which is three wooden posts in the ground behind the "crease".

Ostensibly, the batsman's job is hitting that ball. However, if he hits it, he must run to the opposite wicket to score a "run". He can't really run because he's wearing so much padding and specialist equipment, because the ball is really hard, for no explainable reason. So, the batsman mostly just pretends he will bat, takes the stance of someone fully intending to hit the ball as it flies at him, feigns full commitment to run-scoring, and then, at the last moment, pulls his bat out of the way.

The big tease.

Since so many bowled balls aren't hit, a special man must stand behind the wicket to hoover them all up with his big baseball gloves. He's called a wookie keeper, like in Star Wars.

When this cycle has happened six times, it's the end of the "over." Which is confusing, because for most of the over, *it isn't*. Then it is. Then another over starts and isn't. *Until it is.* This paradox continues until ninety overs are over or everyone got their wicket hit. Then the sides swap jobs. The whole endeavour takes three to five days.

Yes, I said *days*.

If, instead of his bat, the batsman uses his leg to stop the ball from hitting the wicket, he gets in big trouble and people shout "Hoowoowososowoooaoaotat?!" at him. A man called an umpire, who should really be called a referee, decides if the batsman did use his leg, and if he did, he's LBW (lettuce bacon wicket), and that means he's "out". Which is like being over but more final. The man must go inside, where he can eat and drink and google himself and do a million other things more fun than batting.

If the ball is hit, which almost never happens, the batsman can get "runs". If he hits the ball outside the furthest boundary of the pitch, he gets four runs. If the ball doesn't bounce before reaching that boundary, he gets six runs. He gets these automatically, without running.

Weird, right? If he does that three times in a row it's called a "kagoogle" and someone sacrifices a chicken. Hitting the ball with your head is called a "splidgegongy". If you do that, you have to shout "thwackbacky" or you're "pligoting". Harsh, but those are the rules.

The winner is the team that doesn't give up first. Got it? Good.

Once foreigners do understand cricket, their most common reaction is *I don't understand the point of it*.

Well, I can help you with that, too. The point *is* the pointlessness. Cricket is faffing made a sport. Just think about our ancestors, those poor dishevelled malnourished bastards, hunched over all day in a field, hoe in hand, encouraging potatoes to manifest from the ground, like shit wizards, just so that they could extend their lives of horrible, pointless toiling for another day. For fun, they might shoe a horse. Or rip a rotten molar out with their bare hands.

Now, just a few generations later, look at us. Really, stop and look at us. I'll wait . . .

We've got electric toothbrushes, soft ice, car-sharing apps, *weekends*. We've solved so many of the world's problems, got so far down the list of Good Ideas and Nice to Haves and Maybe One Days that we've finally arrived at the very bottom, at cricket.

This is what makes cricket so compelling. It's the sheer arrogance of it. For it to exist, for us to have five days to play it, humanity must have won. Cricket is our celebrating that fact. *Really slowly.* The whole endeavour is sticking two fingers up to the Reaper. Spitting in the face of our own mortality.

That's why we love it.

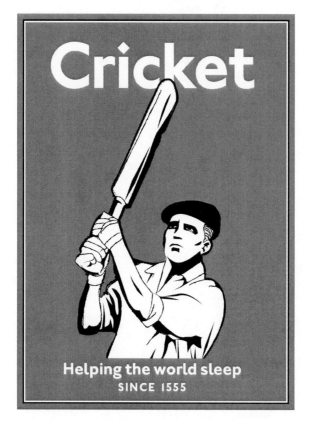

WIMBLEDON

We Brits find Wimbledon ace, smashing, faultless, a real Grand Slam. I'll stop.

But why do we 15–love it so? Last one, I promise.

I think it's because it mashes all the things we enjoy into a big quiche of content: tradition, sport, alcohol, championing an underdog who doesn't triumph, obsessively checking the weather, and, last but in no conceivable way least, *queuing*.

It's a wonder it's only played for a few weeks in June/July and not all year round.

Actually, it's not. Because Wimbledon contains rather a lot of something we don't love: tennis.

Tennis is easily the least interesting part of Wimbledon. Tennis has two good weeks a year, not more. Raise the topic of tennis any time other than June and you won't so much as receive a whimper of enthusiasm, a murmur of interest, a flicker of recognition from my people.

Tennis? Rings a bell. Paddle sport, right?

I'm not even convinced tennis players like tennis. I

think they're just making a rational economic decision because it pays better the being a window cleaner, yoga instructor, or lion tamer.

Not that we'll watch much tennis during those two weeks, of course. Because Wimbledon is about tennis in the same way fishing is about fishing. There might be a little fishing involved in fishing, sometimes, maybe, but it's not mandatory. Fishing is about all the things you aren't doing while you're fishing. *Work. Tax returns. Being with your wife.*

Wimbledon is a coming together, a celebration, an event, a spectacle, a happening.

Sure, maybe from the quarter finals on we'll watch a bit of it on the TV while eating dinner. But for the most part, Wimbledon is a celebration of us, not sport. It's about engaging wholeheartedly in British idiosyncrasies.

You'll know this if you've watched any coverage of it. We devote as little of that to balls being hit as possible. The rest we devote to something far more engaging. Something that really pushes our buttons. A favourite national fetish.

Queueporn—seeing people wasting their mortality in a long, pointless, polite line when they could have just sold their tickets online and saved all the hassle. Hot, sexy, dirty, slow queueporn . . .

Sorry, what was I talking about?

Ah, yes, queues. Wimbledon involves so much queuing that officials even hand out a forty-page booklet to visitors called *A Guide to Queuing*.

Wonderful.

If we need a break from filming the queue, there are plenty of other options: talking to the people in the queue, asking the people in the queue why Wimbledon is so special, filming people eating strawberries on a hill (the name of which is based on whoever our great hope is for that year—it used to be Henman Hill; now it's Murray Mound), and, most important of all, endless, endless shots of the sky. Because tennis is played outdoors, and our outdoors is often wet, which is what adds so much delicious drama to Wimbledon.

Will they be able to play? Will the weather ruin everything again? (Spoiler: yes.)

The average Brit can squeeze an hour's worth of conversation fodder from a single puddle, so imagine what a small-talk bonanza it is for us when the entire sporting world is watching us, watching our skies. Those bemused international viewers probably wonder why we don't just build more retractable roofs, like the one we have now, which was reluctantly added above Wimbledon's famous centre court. If so, they've obviously failed to understand just how little conversation there is in a retractable roof.

THE TYRANNY OF WASPEES

I'm in Berlin, it's summer, and I'm relaxing in a beer garden. There's a slightly plump middle-aged German woman with an aggressively straight fringe sharing a long bench with me. A wasp enters from stage left and begins to buzz around her head. As a Brit, I'm concerned for her safety.

This is a wasp.

This must be taken seriously.

Yet, she does nothing about it. Just sits there as if all is perfectly fine in her world and she's not inches from certain death. As a wasp-avoidance strategy, it seems woefully naive.

"Careful, there's a wasp," I say, as the wasp dives for her nose.

The woman turns to me. She looks me in the eye. She doesn't blink. A second passes. "That's not a wasp, that's a bee," she says, with complete calm. *You've a wasp hugging your eyeball*, I think. *Is this the moment to be a know-all?* And of course, the answer is yes, because this is Germany.

On my funky island, however, this scene would have

played out very differently indeed. Because we Alcopop Drinking Sun Avoiders are utterly, utterly terrified of wasps and bees (waspees, for simplicity's sake). There is no greater overreaction on earth than the overreaction of one of us in their airborne presence. Should one appear— during the three days a year that the weather is good enough to sit outside—and should that waspee get within two metres of us, you better believe all hell will break loose.

It will begin with all the people in the vicinity passing a warning to each other, like impalas on the savannah warning each other of a skulking lion. Cutlery will be dropped. Intimate conversations will cease mid-sentence. ~~Fight~~ Flap-or-flight will kick in. Should the waspee get closer, perhaps dare to land on the edge of a cold glass of Pimm's, we're up, we're waving our arms around, and we're shaking ourselves down.

Get it off. Get it away from us. It's a waspee, God damn it! A waspee!

We're throwing water at it.

We're moving tables.

We're moving inside.

We're trying to trap it in a glass (don't ask).

Or we're in the foetal position, hyperventilating.

It's some shameful shit, even from a culture that's never shied away from overreaction. You saw how we mourned Princess Diana. Well, that's nothing. Little more than a collective shrug compared to how over the top we go in the presence of a flying, stripy sky terrorist.

ROUNDABOUTS

Y ou don't have to travel far in Britain to realise we've been driven round the bend by round-abouts. We've twenty-five thousand of the damn things. The highest proportion of roundabouts to road anywhere in the world. We even have a society called The Roundabout Appreciation Society, where enthusiasts of these mid-road pancakes can meet and discuss . . . *I have no idea*.

"Traffic lights are so fascist and dictatorial, telling you when to stop and go," their leader, Kevin Beresford, told the *Guardian*. Damn right, Kevin—you stick it to those blinking Mussolinis. The organisation's yearly calendar, which contains spectacular full-colour imagery of twelve roundabouts in Redditch, sold one hundred thousand copies worldwide. Although I'm going to guess 99 percent ended up within our shores. In 2013, the association said they were putting a windmill on the front cover to try to attract more female members. Because if there's anything the ladies love, it's windmills (and roundabouts).

We're so into roundabouts, in fact, that we even have

one in Swindon that is five mini-roundabouts inside a giant sixth roundabout crust. It's called The Magic Roundabout, presumably because people who make it through without crashing assume something supernatural has happened. Some of our roundabouts are so big and complex they even have traffic lights—the thing they were supposed to supersede—within them. As logical as putting stairs inside a lift.

We're so crazy about our roundabouts that we've even built an entire city in their homage: Milton Keynes. The Internet—always a bastion of truth in a world of Donald Trump—informs me Milton Keynes has one hundred and thirty such circular intersections. It's part city, part car Waltzer. I went for a job interview there once and came away dizzy, and not because of the miserly salary I was offered.

Why do we love roundabouts so much? There are many theories. City planners and researchers tell us it's because they increase traffic flow and reduce accidents.

That could be true, but let's face it: we've all "had enough of experts . . ."

I think, just as Kevin said, it's because they're a good cultural fit. Instead of being awkward, final, confrontational things like stop signs, junctions, and traffic lights, roundabouts are swirling, inclusive utopias in which everyone is welcome. Even if—as so many utopias are—they're better in concept than execution.

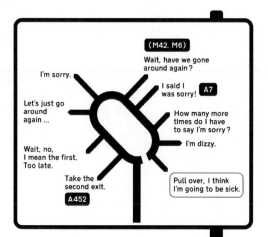

59

BRITAIN'S BIG FREEZE

W hen I was a kid, the most exciting days of all were days when it snowed. My siblings and I would huddle up in our pyjamas and listen to the radio because snow meant school (prison for the prepubescent) might be cancelled. You might not understand how frozen water falling from the sky could close a school, and that's because you're not British. Snow can break anything in our fragile country. It just corrodes things straight through, like acid.

Roads close. Schools close. Fish and chip shops close.

And it's not even real snow, like they have in genuinely frigid places. It's *British snow*. It's like a falling Slush Puppie.

Around this time, an obsession with something called "black ice" begins. It sounds like a Marvel baddie . . . *THIS CAN ONLY HAVE BEEN THE WORK OF BLACK ICE.*

We certainly treat it as something worthy of great fear, yet no one seems to know exactly what black ice is. I suspect because it doesn't exist. It's the yeti of weather. Every summer for the last twenty years, the news has warned us of an incoming invasion of African bees.

Black ice is that, for winter.

Regardless, the nation hunkers down and waits for this nefarious white wizard to pass, glued to a news channel talking exclusively about the snow, all other news having been frozen out. Camerapeople have been on the streets since dawn icing the pavements, just so they can get footage of elderly people falling over.

When will the chaos end? What does the snow want from us? How many will die? These questions grip the nation.

I brought this SNOW TERROR mentality with me when I moved to Leipzig. Then it snowed. I rushed to the kitchen. I sat down. I listened to the radio. There was nothing about the snow. It was just same old Depeche Mode this, Ace of Base that, as if 1992 had never left us.

I didn't even get the day off work.

Life just carried on as normal.

Now I live in Berlin, where some years we've fifty centimetres of snow packed up by the side of the road for weeks. We just walk next to it in specialised footwear, as if it's not even there. As if it might not contain deadly black ice. As if life is still normal. AS IF IT'S NOT SNOWING!

We have the expression "Water off a duck's back", which means "No big deal". I'd like to lobby for it to be changed to "Frozen water off a German's back". Because snow is just nothing to these people. They prepare. They change their summer tyres to winter ones. They have world-class windows. They put on specialised clothing. We don't even have the concept of winter tyres. Our windows are a see-through gesture, at best. At most, we might think about putting on a pair of tights under our mini-skirts. It's like we want to be completely surprised by winter every year. Almost as if we want to have an excuse not to go to work.

Wait, hang on a minute . . .

60

"IF YOU DON'T LIKE IT, I'VE GOT THE RECIPT."

G ift giving is a social minefield in every culture. The whole ritual is fraught with opportunities to offend, compliment, draw attention to yourself, and show emotion.

In short, all the things Brits hate.

It's probably no surprise how bad we are at it, then. In German, *gift* means "poison". I think they're on to something. Just in case you have to give us a present, or receive one from us, I'll now explain the steps in this complex maze of British obligation.

1. The gifter is required to present the giftee with both a gift and a card.

2. The giftee *must* open the card first. The card is pointless and serves only as a way of extending the gift-giving ceremony. Paper foreplay.

3. The giftee must open the card and study it closely. If there is a joke on the card—97 percent of the time there will be a joke on the card—the poorness of said joke must be ignored and the giftee must release a hearty belly laugh for at least twenty seconds, while crying at least one tear.

4. The giftee must carefully place the boring card on her lap. She now holds the present. The main event.

5. While the gift is still wrapped, the gifter is required to destroy it verbally, thus lowering expectations of it. Acceptable phrases are "It's just a silly little thing, really", "I don't know what I was thinking", or "I don't even really know why I got it".

This step *must* then end with the gifter saying this exact phrase: "If you don't like it, I've got the receipt." Failure to do so causes a rip in the space-time continuum, killing us all.

6. Now that expectations have been lowered, and the present is still wrapped, the giftee must now begin defending the present, despite not knowing what it is: "I'm sure it's lovely", "If it's from you, I'll like it", or, "You always give such lovely gifts".

7. The giftee should now attempt to guess what the present is. Note: The giftee is not allowed to get it right. For this would pop the ceremony's balloon prematurely. If, from the shape, it's obviously a book, for example, acceptable guesses are "Inflatable yurt?", "Yangtze River dolphin?" or, "George Foreman Lean Mean Fat Reducing Grilling Machine?"

8. The gifter must then smile, demurely, but reveal nothing.

9. The giftee may now begin slowly opening the present from one corner.

10. The giftee will fail to open the present because the gifter has cellotaped it to within an inch of its life, making it to sticky tape what the Sistine Chapel is to ceiling art.

11. The giftee, with the help of the gifter, and increasing aggressiveness, should free a corner of the present from the wrapping.

12. At this juncture, the giftee is required to guess once

more. While it is not mandatory to be wrong, it is encouraged. If you know for sure it's a book, acceptable second guesses are "Rectangular Frisbee?", "DVD box set?" or "Shopping list anthology?!"

While it goes without saying, for the particularly socially hare-brained, I'll say it anyway: the giftee should not, <u>under any circumstances</u>, guess something of greater financial value than the actual gift. *Dick move.*

13. The rest of the wrapping can now be removed. The present can be revealed. Now a tricky phase begins. The giftee must match the negativity set by the gifter in step 5 with a greater amount of positivity. "Brilliant. Fantastic. Great. Thanks! You really shouldn't have"—this should suffice for a first pass.

14. The giver must then feign doubt about the appropriateness of all this praise, saying something along the lines of "Does it fit okay? Oh god, you hate it, don't you? You can tell me. Be honest! Do you hate it? I HAVE THE RECEIPT!"

15. The giftee is then required to meet this escalation with an even more bombastic praise-wave, regardless of the quality of the present. "Hate it? It's my heart's desire. In many ways, receiving this gift is the pinnacle of my life thus far. I mean, who doesn't love *socks?*"

16. Having narrowly avoided a friendship-ending booby trap, the giftee can put the present down, hug the gifter, and rejoice in knowing it's another 365 days until her next birthday.

BARGAINS

It's not only gift giving that we Banter Bards do weirdly. We also shop in an odd, illogical fashion. We don't enter retail establishments with a list of things we need and compare the attributes of the items offered against that list.

Problem then solution. This would be commendable. But it's not the way of my people.

We don't shop for specific items. We shop for bargains.

If we do have a problem to solve, it's *having money*, which, fortunately, the solution of shopping is always happy to help fix for us. Our discount fixation means we're not just casual browsers killing time on a Saturday afternoon—we're appraisers, surveyors, discount detectives, sale sleuths hunting the high street for the deal of the century! Say we enter a shop and find a slightly weird, dusty, off-pink, fluffy jumper that was sixty-four pounds but has been reduced to the unbelievable price of just fourteen pounds. Someone not raised in our culture might point out to us that it is:

A) Nothing we would ever have considered buying at sixty-four pounds.

B) Nothing anyone would have considered buying at sixty-four pounds, hence the discount.

C) Still overpriced at fourteen pounds.

D) Ugly as sin.

Don't. This is our thing. You've probably heard of beer goggles—which make the opposite sex become more attractive. Well, we Brits have bargain goggles. Through these distorted lenses of WANT and NOW, that jumper appears to us as fourteen pounds' worth of pure, undiluted, unrestrained, unbelievable YES. That's because our bargain goggles blur the before and after price, drawing attention instead to the THE GAP between them.

Saving fifty pounds? On one item? And getting a jumper out of it? Incredible! A slightly weird, dusty, off-pink, fluffy jumper, but let's not focus on that. We won't focus on that.

Of course, there are no bargains. The whole concept is fundamentally flawed, like a bridge of custard. As if the store owners say, at some predictable point in the year, "How much have we made? That's enough, isn't it? Did the CEO get his new yacht? Did we give our workers in Bangladesh a pay rise? Terrific. Then let's give something back to the British people. Sell it all at lower than cost. Come on. Do it. Roll the dice. Screw profit."

But in that moment, in the heady rush of the sale, with our bargain goggles on, we forget this. We even had one store called Officer's Club, whose business model was designed specifically to exploit our national obsession/passion/myopia. Everything in the store was always on sale, reduced by at least 70 percent. Legally, they had to have one store in their chain sell the items at the full price, prob-

169

ably open just an hour every second Tuesday. This allowed all the other stores to pretend their discounts were genuine.

We would have to pretend, too, of course. We were ready to pretend. So ready.

They even got as high as 90 percent off at one point. Who can resist a 90 percent reduction?

Not us, that's for sure.

My family used to get up early to "go to the sales" on Boxing Day each year. Some of the sales would start at 7am. The traffic would be chaos, as all the other bargain-believing delusionals were also flocking to the nearest shopping mall to hunt out a "right bargain" on a DVD box set of *Friends* or pair of green jeans. Only now do I recognise the absurdity of it. It seemed so normal back then.

Our love of bargains is so strong, and our shamelessness so great, that we will even take things back (including gifts) and re-buy them if we find them reduced in a sale. Yeah, really. We know our statutory rights and that with every heavily discounted purchase, we undermine capitalism. We win. *MWWWWWWHHHHHHHHHHHHHHHHH-HHHHHHHHHHHH . . .*

HUNTING

BARGAIN HUNTING

IT'S A LONDON THING

"When a man is tired of London, he is tired of life; for there is in London all that life can afford," said Samuel Johnson. Which might have been true when he said it in 1777. If he was still there in 2017, sitting in a damp, mouldy bedsit in zone 6—a bedsit that he shared with four other people, that had no heating and a leaking roof, and that sat above a Domino's Pizza—he'd change his mind pretty sharpish.

We Brits have a difficult relationship with London. We want to love it. It's our capital. Flagship Britain (or England, at least). People throw around phrases such as "steeped in history" cheaply, but London is truly deserving of them. It has buildings older than many countries. Not that this codger has had its day in the ~~sun~~ drizzle just yet; the London of today is still the apex of our politics, power, economy, and culture. A place where anything is possible. Where if you want to naked-tango-yoga-mediation-tantra-dance at 7:45 on a wet Tuesday night in March, you can do that. There will be four separate meetups for it. You don't even need to book ahead. London has everything you could possibly want, buried below six feet of all the things that you don't: congestion, pollution, crime, extortionate prices, chavs, low-quality housing, long commutes, seven-pound sandwiches.

After uni, everyone packed up their little cars and headed straight for London—the only place hiring. There they found their standard of living had actually decreased. If they thought they'd been poor before, now they truly knew poverty, paying three times as much rent for half the square metres and quadruple the commute.

London today is, paradoxically, both the place to be and the place only oil sheiks can afford to be.

You've probably heard that London has a congestion charge, but you probably didn't know it applies to everyone inside the city limits, at all times, including you, should you visit. Every forty-five minutes, neo-liberal capitalist ninjas silently relieve you of your wallet/purse, remove five pounds from it, then put it back without your noticing. Every evening you look inside and think, *Where did all my money go?*

Wallet congestion charge.

London also seems to exist in some sort of Bermuda Travel Triangle where every journey takes one hour, regardless of whether you go one Tube stop or fifteen. Some countries had the smart sense to decentralise, to share their industry out across their geography. We elected to put all our eggs into this one regional basket. As a result, today, it's an economic octopus slowly wrapping more of its tentacles around the nation, strangling the autonomy out of other regions.

But what an octopus! London is the best of us, the worst of us, and, because of its cost, contains ever fewer of us.

TRANSPORT TUG OF WAR

We Brits like to behave as if there's a fifty-centimetre social force field around us at all times. That's why we're such natural queuers. Without the conformity of the queue, there'd just be a big jumble of people getting near enough to rub themselves on each other.

In a queue, however, we can orientate, like birds in a flock, since we need only keep an eye on the person in front of us. It's a huge relief. Problems arise, however, when we must enter an enclosed space—a space where we're forced to be near other people. Public transport, for example.

Our force field doesn't work on public transport. There's just not enough space. Instead, we become reluctant participants in transport tug of war—a game where our desire for space must show its strength, must out-muscle our pathological politeness.

Ready to play transport tug of war? Here we go.

You've entered a bus. As a Brit you will, instinctively, immediately scan the area to see where the most space is, considering also how far that space is from the driver and the likelihood of drunks, gropers, masturbators, chavs, and the hygiene stunted being on this line at this time of day.

As luck has it, you find a free two-seater halfway down the bus. Excellent work.

Upon arrival at the aforementioned two-seater, you have two choices: aisle seat or window seat. Window offers a better view but increases the odds someone will sit next to you, because he could do so without inconveniencing you. He'd simply have to ask, "Is this seat free?" already knowing that it is, and suddenly the two of you are seat mates.

What if the person who sits there is crazy, smells bad, or, even worse, talks about his feelings? You'll be trapped in against the window, forced to listen. You might even start talking about your feelings. You could move to another seat, but that would be a drastic act of character assassination. Just alighting will be problematic enough, for you'll have to ask this person to move without touching him or looking him too forcefully in the eye.

A social minefield, the stress of which might mire the remainder of the journey.

Regardless of which seat you choose, you must now work to keep the seat next to you free. You do this by placing your bags upon it. If you have no bags, find something else to place upon it. A magazine? A half-eaten crisp sandwich? A shoe?

A shoe!

Not a minute too soon, as the bus is filling up now. There are no blocks of two seats left. Pretend you haven't noticed that. Put your headphones in. Stare out of the window. Look mean. Look at your phone. Look at your ~~shoes~~ shoe. Who's that coming down the aisle? One of the lower social classes? Is that the sound of tinny rap music being played on a mobile phone? Oh no.

Not you . . . Not you . . . Not your seat . . . Look away . . . Look away . . .

Phew, he sat two seats further down, next to some other poor schmuck.

You brave a quick glance around. There are hardly any free seats now. There's a pang in your chest. It's your British conscience, which is like other consciences, but eight times as pangy.

Should you remove your shoe and free up the seat?

This is a personal question. An ethical choice. You'll have to spend the rest of the day with yourself, a task made easier if you can convince yourself you're a nice person. You check your social karma: you bought a copy of the *Big Issue* earlier; you called your grandmother last Tuesday; you once righted an upside-down tortoise. Your balance is positive, you're sure. You hold firm.

But then the next person coming down the aisle is a sweet old lady. You don't want anyone next to you, sure, but if it must be someone, you'll take her—harmless, hard of hearing, easy to outrun. You quickly remove your stuff and smile at her.

She walks right past you, the ungrateful wench. You curse her, silently. Behind her comes a teenage girl showered in fake tan. You quickly put your stuff back down. You look back out of the window. She passes, too. Why? What's wrong with you? You sniff your armpits.

Fine. Lavender.

A middle-aged woman with a tight bob approaches. You do not smile. Not after Oldwomangate. You are firm. You are not nice. You smell bad. You illegally download.

You look down. She hesitates. She knows she must ask someone if she can sit down. She's evaluating who looks the nicest, the safest, the least crazy. She stands before you. You evaluate if it's a good moment to pretend you have Tourette's. You do not pretend you have Tourette's.

"Excuse me, do you mind if I sit there?" she asks.

You act completely surprised by the knowledge that there's a seat next to you. *Has this been there this whole time? Really? And new people have gotten on the bus and want a seat? When did all this happen? I had no idea. Just no idea. Oh, someone put a shoe on it. That's strange. I'll just remove it.*

You smile politely. "Of course," you say, swivelling so that she can get in.

You curse her, in your head.

"Thank you," she says, sitting down, cursing you in her head.

"No problem," you say, as if it weren't obvious to you both that you were the one who made the problem in the first place. You put your shoe back on. You do not talk further.

One stop early, because you accidentally pressed the button too soon but were too embarrassed to tell the driver that, you get off the bus. You thank the driver as if he's done you an impossibly large favour. Everyone will.

Transport tug of war is over, for today.

The How British Are You? Quiz

To conclude this little tome, here's a quiz that will allow you to put all you've learned into action. Finally, after all those days and nights of wondering, you will learn how British you are.

You'll need either a remarkably good memory or a piece of paper. There are ten questions, with four choices each. The points follow the quiz. No peeking.

Good luck!

Q1. At the hair salon, you've been given a terrible haircut that makes you look like a deranged baboon. The hairdresser holds the mirror up and asks what you think. You:

A: Change the subject ("How about this weather we've been having?").

B: Tell the truth ("I'm terribly sorry, but you've made me look like a deranged baboon. Could you fix it, please? If it's not too much bother. Thanks.").

C: Lie a little bit ("Erm. Ummm. Well. Ahh. Yes. It definitely makes a statement, doesn't it? Perhaps it could make a little bit less of one? Thanks.").

D: Lie a lot ("Lovely. You've done a terrific job.") then walk to the next hair salon, sit down, and start the whole process again.

Q2. I say "British", you say . . .

A: "Bulldog!"
B: "*Bake Off*!"
C: "Empire!"
D: "Airways!"

Q3. It's morning and you've been out of bed for one hour. How many cups of tea have you had to drink?

A: You've lost count.
B: 1–2
C: 3+
D: 0. Tea is overrated.

Q4. You are British. You have a problem. What is the solution?

A: The mass consumption of humour. Make fun of the problem, yourself, life, and the universe.
B: The mass consumption of tea.
C: The mass consumption of Cadbury chocolate.
D: The mass consumption of alcohol.

Q5. Your neighbours often play loud music, and they have a scruffy garden. This annoys you. What do you do about it?

A: Post them an anonymous passive-aggressive note.
B: Invite them over for a BBQ, during which you repeatedly make comments about the
loud music and scruffy garden of another neighbour, hoping they get the hint.
C: Smile and wave every time you see them (aka nothing).
D: Give them an offensive nickname (Loudy McLouter-

son?) and complain bitterly about them to everyone else but say nothing to them.

Q6. You are trapped on a deserted island. A genie appears and offers you an unlimited supply of one food item. What do you pick?

A: Fish and chips.
B: Yorkshire pudding.
C: Cadbury Mini Eggs.
D: Greggs' sausage rolls.

Q7. It's twenty-two degrees Celsius outside. The sun appears, momentarily, from behind a cloud. What do you do?

A: Complain bitterly that it's now too hot.
B: Nothing. Normal life will resume shortly, you're sure.
C: Stare up at the sky in confusion. Where did this big orange sky Frisbee come from? Why is it on fire?
D: Immediately remove as many items of clothing as polite company allows. Bathe in factor-thirty suntan lotion. Refuse to go back inside until you are part-human, part-lobster.

Q8. Which word or phrase best describes your relationship to Marmite?

A: Indifferent.
B: Overwhelmingly negative.
C: Lukewarm.
D: Passionately positive.

Q9. It's June, which means it's time for Wimbledon. What most excites you about this event?

A: Drinking the British sangria, aka Pimm's.
B: Queueporn— dirty, dirty queueporn. All those people queuing for hours. Trying to get a ticket. *Mmmm. Yeah.* Look at them. Very arousing.
C: Watching world-class tennis.
D: Eating strawberries and cream.

Q10. You have been run over by an ice-cream truck. You lie bleeding profusely on the road. A piano falls from the sky onto your head. All your bitcoins are stolen by a Moldavian hacker. It begins to rain. A paramedic arrives and asks how you are. What do you say?

A: "Finethanksandyou?"
B: "I've been better."
C: "HOW THE F}%^ DO YOU THINK I AM?"
D: "I could do without the rain."

The Scores

Q1. A: 2pts B: 1pt C: 3pts D: 4pts
Q2. A: 3pts B: 4pts C: 2pts D: 1pt
Q3. A: 4pts B: 2pts C: 3pts D: 1pt
Q4. A: 4pts B: 1pt C: 2pts D: 3pts
Q5. A: 1pt B: 2pt C: 3pts D: 4pts
Q6. A: 1pt B: 4pts C: 2pts D: 3pts
Q7. A: 3pts B: 1pt C: 2pts D: 4pts
Q8. A: 1pt B: 3pts C: 2pts D: 4pts
Q9. A: 3pts B: 4pts C: 1pt D: 2pms
Q10. A: 3pts B: 2pts C: 1pt D: 4pts*

*I know, back in Chapter 3, I told you the correct answer in a scenario like this is "finethanksandyou". That's a strong answer, hence the 3pts, but I think "I could do without the rain" has an unexpected comedic whimsy that just pips it. *Sorry.*

Add up your points and discover whether you're . . .

. . . *as British as the French* (**0–20 points**):
Rubbish! Have you even been to our damp collection of islands? Do you even like tea? When was the last time you made an inordinate fuss out of doing something small and inconsequential, such as opening the window on a train? Ages ago, probably.

Go back to the start of the book and begin again.

. . . *as British as a pork pie* (**21–25 points**):
You were trying, I guess, just about. But you're still far too direct, too polite, too sober, too reluctant to overcomplicate

everything in the pursuit of niceness. You've not watched a single minute of *Bake Off*, have you? I thought not.

You have work to do. Get to it.

. . . *as British as an unnecessary apology* (26–31 points):

Bloody marvellous! You drink your tea milky, you don't make a scene, you're obsessively polite, you martyr, and you swear like a drunken sailor. You blend in reasonably well with the British—congratulations. But that doesn't mean you can't improve, of course. Have you considered a little more faffing? When did you last eat a chip butty? Or got out of the lift two floors early and took the stairs because someone else got in and it was awkward?

Complacency is your enemy. Do not let it win.

. . . *as British as the Queen* (32–40 points):

You've done pretty bloody spiffing, I say. You're a real chip off Blighty's block. You're as British as crumpets, biscuits, and hiding behind a bush to avoid talking to someone. No matter what your passport says, your heart beats Britannia.

Jolly good show, old chap!

Last But Not Least

I hope you've enjoyed this irreverent guide to us Marmite Munchers. If so, I have only one recommendation (assuming you're not already amongst us): come visit! We're much friendlier and more hospitable than recent political developments might suggest. And we're lost over here, on our damp little islands, under our Masks of Civility, small talking the day away, failing to live up to the Ideal of Britishness. Come and distract us from ourselves. I can't promise you'll understand us, but I can promise you'll be entertained by us (if it's no inconvenience, sorry to be a bother, and no problem if not, etc., etc.).

We'll have the kettle on, banter prepared, and a crisp sandwich waiting.

Thanks for reading!

How much would you risk to change your life?

If you enjoyed this book, I have several more that I'm very proud of. I'd suggest you start with my book Don't Go There, in which I go to places everyone else is trying to get away from. Places like North Korea, Chernobyl, Transnistria and Liberland (the newest country in the world). What I learn there threatens my threatens my world view, sanity, and relationship.

It's full of interesting characters, uncomfortable moments, unusual destinations, and British humour that will appeal to lovers of Bill Bryson, Douglas Adams, and David Sedaris. It has been an Amazon travel bestseller for months with really positive reviews. It's also laughably cheap.

You can find it at your local Amazon.

Made in United States
North Haven, CT
30 December 2023

46707912R00114